WHAT'S COOKING

barbecue

Salads for Summer

Jacqueline Bellefontaine

This is a Parragon Book
This edition published in 2002

Parragon
Queen Street House
4 Queen Street
Bath BA1 1HE, UK

ISBN: 0-75258-533-9

Printed in China

Produced by Haldane Mason, London

Acknowledgements
Art Director: Ron Samuels
Editorial Director: Sydney Francis
Editorial Consultant: Christopher Fagg
Managing Editor: Jo-Anne Cox
Editor: Lydia Darbyshire
Design: Digital Artworks Partnership Ltd
Photography: St John Asprey
Home Economist: Jacqueline Bellefontaine

Note
Cup measurements in this book are for American cups.
Tablespoons are assumed to be 15 ml. Unless otherwise stated,
milk is assumed to be full fat, eggs are standard size 3
and pepper is freshly ground pepper.

The barbecues used for the photography in this book were kindly supplied by:
Weber, Yardley Road, Knowsley Industrial Park North, Kirkby, Liverpool L33 7SS
and Castle Catering Supplies, 4 King James Court, London SE1.

Contents

Introduction

What is it that makes a meal cooked outdoors over burning coals so appetizing? Perhaps it's the fresh air or the tantalizing aroma or the sound of food sizzling on the cooking rack. Whatever it is, there is no doubt that barbecues (grills) are becoming more and more popular. This is hardly surprising when you see just how many wonderful dishes can be cooked over charcoal. This book alone contains 120 recipes, leaving you with no shortage of inspiration.

Gone are the days when sausages and burgers were the staple of every barbecue (grill) party, although traditionalists will find recipes here for making fabulous burgers and for tangy sauces to serve with the sausages. But why not try fish, which cooks to perfection on the barbecue (grill) and is healthy too? There are also dozens of tasty marinades and bastes for meat lovers, as well as vegetarian dishes, salads and side dishes. You can even cook a dessert on the barbecue (grill).

WHICH BARBECUE (GRILL)?

You do not need a large, sophisticated barbecue (grill) to produce mouthwatering food, although once you have tried some of these recipes you might want to invest in something larger.

Essentially barbecues (grills) are an open fire with a rack set over the hot coals, on which the food is cooked. You can improvise a makeshift barbecue (grill) with nothing more complicated than a few house bricks and an old oven rack. **Chicken wire** and **baking racks** can also be used to cook on. Purpose-made barbecues (grills) are, however, available in all shapes and sizes, from small disposable trays to large wagon, gas-powered models.

As the names suggest, **portable** and **semi-portable barbecues (grills)** tend to be small. Some types have a stand or folding legs; others have fixed legs. If you have a small model and are cooking for large numbers, cook the food in rotation so that guests can begin on the first course while the second batch is cooking.

Most **brazier barbecues (grills)**, which stand on long legs and have a wind shield, are light and portable. On some models the height of the rack can be varied, and some types incorporate rotisseries.

Covered barbecues (grills) are essential if you want to cook whole joints of meat. The lid completely covers the barbecue (grill), increasing the temperature at which food cooks and acting, in effect, like an oven. The temperature is controlled by air vents. When used without the cover, these barbecues (grills) are treated like traditional barbecues (grills).

Wagon barbecues (grills) are larger and more sophisticated. They have wheels and often incorporate a tabletop.

Electric or **gas barbecues (grills)** heat volcanic lava coals. The flavour is still good, because the flavour of barbecued (grilled) food comes from the aromas of fat and juices burning on the coals rather than the fuel itself.

EQUIPMENT

Apart from the barbecue (grill) itself, you do not need any special equipment, but do arm yourself with a pair of **oven gloves (potholders)**. **Long-handled tools** can be useful, as well as being safer and more convenient to use. They are not expensive, and if you cook on a barbecue (grill) regularly it is a good idea to invest in a set. **Racks** for burgers, sausages and fish are useful but not essential.

You will need a set of **skewers** if you want to cook kebabs (kabobs). *Metal skewers* should be flat to stop the food slipping round as it cooks. Remember that metal skewers get very hot, so wear gloves (potholders) or use *tongs* to turn them. *Wooden skewers* are much cheaper than metal skewers but are not always very long lasting. Always soak wooden skewers in cold water for at least 30 minutes before use to help prevent them from burning on the barbecue (grill) and then cover the exposed ends with pieces of kitchen foil.

A **water spray** is useful for cooling down coals or dampening down flare-ups.

LIGHTING THE BARBECUE (GRILL)

Charcoal is the most popular fuel although you can use wood. Charcoal is available as *lump wood*, which is irregular in shape and size but easy to light, or as *briquettes*, which burn for longer and with a more uniform heat but are harder to light.

Light the barbecue (grill) at least an hour before you want to start cooking. Stack the coals in the pan and use specially designed solid or liquid lighter fuels to help set the charcoal alight. Do not use household fire lighters because these will taint the food. Never use paraffin or petrol to light a barbecue (grill) – it can be very dangerous if used incorrectly.

The barbecue (grill) is ready to use when the flames have died down and the coals are covered with a white ash. When the coals are ready, spread them out into a uniform layer.

PREPARING TO COOK

Before you begin to cook, oil the rack so that the food does not stick to it. Do this away from the barbecue (grill) or the oil will flare up as it drips on to the coals. For most dishes, position the rack about 7.5 cm/ 3 inches above the coals. Raise the rack if you want to slow down the cooking. If you cannot adjust the height of the rack, slow down the cooking by spreading out the coals or moving the food to the edges of the rack, where the heat will be less intense.

If your barbecue (grill) has air vents, use them to control the temperature – open the vents for more heat, close them to reduce the temperature.

It is very difficult to give exact times for cooking on a barbecue (grill), so use the times given in the recipes in this book as a guide only. Always test the food to make sure that it is cooked throughly before serving.

Fish & Seafood

Fish tastes wonderful when it is cooked on the barbecue (grill). This chapter is full of ideas, ranging from simple char-grilled whole fish to spicy marinated parcels and kebabs (kabobs). Oily fish is especially suitable for the barbecue (grill) because the flesh does not dry out over the direct heat. White fish will benefit from the addition of a baste or marinade if it is cooked directly over the coals, but smaller fish can be cooked whole, because the skin keeps in all the wonderful juices and acts as a natural protective coating. Barbecue (grill) fish steaks with a marinade or baste direct on the rack.

Choose a fish with a firm flesh or it may break up and drop on to the coals when you turn it. Alternatively, invest in hinged rack, which will make turning infinitely easier. A firm fish, such as monkfish, is essential for skewers, and wrap more delicate fish in kitchen foil, so that it cooks in its own juice.

Seafood is quick to cook and does not need to be left in a marinade for long, making it ideal for impromptu barbecues (grills). Prawn (shrimp) skewers, for example, can be made and cooked in minutes.

Indonesian-style Spicy Cod

A delicious aromatic coating makes this dish rather special.
Serve it with a crisp salad and crusty bread.

Serves 4

INGREDIENTS

4 cod steaks
1 stalk lemon grass
1 small red onion, chopped
3 cloves garlic, chopped
2 fresh red chillies, deseeded and
  chopped

1 tsp grated root (fresh) ginger
1/4 tsp turmeric
2 tbsp butter, cut into small cubes
8 tbsp canned coconut milk
2 tbsp lemon juice

salt and pepper
red chillies, to garnish (optional)

1 Rinse the cod steaks and pat them dry on absorbent kitchen paper.

2 Remove and discard the outer leaves from the lemon grass and thinly slice the inner section.

3 Place the lemon grass, onion, garlic, chilli, ginger and turmeric in a food processor and blend until the ingredients are finely chopped. Season with salt and pepper to taste.

4 With the processor running, add the butter, coconut milk and lemon juice and process until well blended.

5 Place the fish in a shallow, non-metallic dish. Pour over the coconut mixture and turn the fish until well coated.

6 If you have one, place the fish steaks in a hinged basket, which will make them easier to turn. Barbecue (grill) over hot coals for 15 minutes or until the fish is cooked through, turning once. Serve garnished with red chillies, if wished.

COOK'S TIP

If you prefer a milder flavour omit the chillies altogether. For a hotter flavour do not remove the seeds from the chillies.

Blackened Fish

The word 'blackened' refers to the spicy marinade that is used to coat the fish and that chars slightly as it cooks. Choose a fish with a firm texture, such as hake or halibut.

Serves 4

INGREDIENTS

4 white fish steaks
1 tbsp paprika
1 tsp dried thyme
1 tsp cayenne pepper

1 tsp freshly ground black pepper
$1/2$ tsp freshly ground white pepper
$1/2$ tsp salt
$1/4$ tsp ground allspice

50 g/$1^3/4$ oz unsalted butter
3 tbsp sunflower oil

1 Rinse the fish steaks and pat them dry with absorbent kitchen paper.

2 Mix together the paprika, thyme, cayenne peppers, black and white peppers, salt and allspice in a shallow dish.

3 Place the butter and oil in a small saucepan and heat, stirring occasionally, until the butter melts.

4 Brush the butter mixture liberally all over the fish steaks, on both sides.

5 Dip the fish into the spicy mix until well coated on both sides.

6 Barbecue (grill) the fish over hot coals for about 10 minutes on each side, turning once. Continue to baste the fish with the remaining butter mixture during the cooking time.

COOK'S TIP

Basting the fish with the butter mixture will ensure that the fish remains moist during cooking.

VARIATION

A whole fish - red mullet, for example - rather than steaks is also delicious cooked this way. The spicy seasoning can also be used to coat chicken portions, if you prefer.

Monkfish Skewers with Courgettes (Zucchini) & Lemon

A simple basting sauce is brushed over these tasty kebabs (kabobs),
which make a perfect light meal on their own.

Serves 4

INGREDIENTS

450 g/1 lb monkfish tail
2 courgettes (zucchini)
1 lemon
12 cherry tomatoes
8 bay leaves

SAUCE:
4 tbsp olive oil
2 tbsp lemon juice
1 tsp chopped, fresh thyme
$1/2$ tsp lemon pepper
salt

TO SERVE:
green salad leaves
fresh, crusty bread

1 Cut the monkfish into 5 cm/ 2 inch chunks. Cut the courgettes (zucchini) into thick slices and the lemon into wedges.

2 Thread the monkfish, courgettes (zucchini), lemon, tomatoes and bay leaves on to 4 skewers.

3 To make the basting sauce, combine the oil, lemon juice, thyme, lemon pepper and salt to taste in a small bowl.

4 Brush the basting sauce liberally all over the fish, lemon, tomatoes and bay leaves on the skewers.

5 Cook the skewers on the barbecue (grill) for about 15 minutes, basting frequently with the sauce, until the fish is cooked through.

6 Serve the kebabs with green salad leaves and warm, fresh crusty bread.

VARIATION

Use plaice (flounder) fillets instead of the monkfish, if you prefer. Allow two fillets per person, and skin and cut each fillet lengthwise into two. Roll up each piece and thread them on to the skewers.

Monkfish Skewers with Coconut & Coriander (Cilantro)

This is a tasty kebab (kabob) with a mild marinade. Allow the skewers to marinate for at least an hour before cooking.

Serves 4

INGREDIENTS

450 g/1 lb monkfish tails
225 g/8 oz uncooked peeled prawns (shrimp)
desiccated (shredded) coconut, toasted, to garnish (optional)

MARINADE:
1 tsp sunflower oil
$1/2$ small onion, finely grated
1 tsp root (fresh) ginger, grated

150 ml/5 fl oz/$2/3$ cup canned coconut milk
2 tbsp chopped, fresh coriander (cilantro)

1 To make the marinade, heat the oil in a wok or saucepan and fry the onion and ginger for 5 minutes until just softened but not browned.

2 Add the coconut milk to the pan and bring to the boil. Boil rapidly for about 5 minutes or until reduced to the consistency of single (light) cream.

3 Remove the pan from the heat and allow to cool completely. Once cooled, stir in the coriander (cilantro) and pour into a shallow dish.

4 Cut the fish into bite-sized chunks and stir gently into the coconut mixture together with the prawns (shrimp). Leave to chill in the refrigerator for 1–4 hours.

5 Thread the fish and prawns (shrimp) on to skewers and discard any remaining marinade. Barbecue (grill) the skewers over hot coals for 10–15 minutes, turning frequently. Garnish with toasted coconut, if wished.

VARIATION

Look out for uncooked prawns (shrimp) in the freezer cabinet in large supermarkets. If you cannot obtain them, you can use cooked prawns (shrimp), but remember they only need heating through.

Charred Tuna Steaks

*Tuna has a firm flesh, which is ideal for barbecuing (grilling),
but it can be a little dry unless it is marinated first.*

Serves 4

INGREDIENTS

4 tuna steaks
3 tbsp soy sauce
1 tbsp Worcestershire sauce
1 tsp wholegrain mustard

1 tsp caster (superfine) sugar
1 tbsp sunflower oil
green salad, to serve

TO GARNISH:
flat-leaf parsley
lemon wedges

1 Place the tuna steaks in a shallow dish.

2 Mix together the soy sauce, Worcestershire sauce, mustard, sugar and oil in a small bowl. Pour the marinade over the tuna steaks.

3 Gently turn over the tuna steaks, using your fingers or a fork, so that they are well coated with the marinade.

4 Cover and place the tuna steaks in the refrigerator and leave to chill for between 30 minutes and 2 hours.

5 Barbecue (grill) the marinated fish over hot coals for 10–15 minutes, turning once. Baste frequently with any of the marinade that is left in the dish.

6 Garnish with flat-leaf parsley and lemon wedges, and serve with a fresh green salad.

COOK'S TIP

If a marinade contains soy sauce, the marinating time should be limited, usually to 2 hours. If allowed to marinate for too long, the fish will dry out and become tough.

COOK'S TIP

Tuna has a dark red flesh, which turns paler on cooking. Tuna has a good meaty texture, but if you are unable to obtain it, use swordfish steaks instead.

Char-grilled Bream

Bream have quite tough scales, which need to be removed before cooking.
Ask the fishmonger to do this for you. A single sea bream is the ideal size for one person.

Serves 2

INGREDIENTS

2 small sea bream, scaled, gutted,
   trimmed and cleaned
2 slices lemon
2 bay leaves
salt and pepper

BASTE:
4 tbsp olive oil
2 tbsp lemon juice
$1/2$ tsp chopped, fresh oregano
$1/2$ tsp chopped, fresh thyme

TO GARNISH:
fresh bay leaves
fresh thyme sprig
lemon wedges

1 Using a sharp knife, cut 2–3 deep slashes into the bodies of both fish in order to help them fully absorb the flavour of the basting sauce.

2 Place a slice of lemon and a bay leaf inside the cavity of each fish. Season inside the cavity with salt and pepper.

3 In a small bowl, mix together the ingredients for the baste using a fork. Alternatively, place the basting ingredients in a small screw-top jar and shake well to combine.

4 Brush some of the baste liberally over the fish and place them on a rack over hot coals. Barbecue (grill) over hot coals for 20-30 minutes, turning and basting frequently.

5 Transfer the fish to a serving plate, garnish with fresh bay leaves, thyme and lemon wedges and serve.

VARIATION

If you prefer, use brill or a fish like gurnand instead of the sea bream.

COOK'S TIP

The flavour of the dish will be enhanced if you use good fresh ingredients in the sauce. Dried herbs can be used, but remember that the flavour is much more intense, so only use half the quantity of the fresh herbs listed above.

Salmon Yakitori

The Japanese sauce used here combines well with salmon, although it is usually served with chicken.

Serves 4

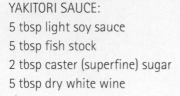

INGREDIENTS

350 g/12 oz chunky salmon fillet
8 baby leeks

YAKITORI SAUCE:
5 tbsp light soy sauce
5 tbsp fish stock
2 tbsp caster (superfine) sugar
5 tbsp dry white wine

3 tbsp sweet sherry
1 clove garlic, crushed

1 Skin the salmon and cut the flesh into 5 cm/2 inch chunks. Trim the leeks and cut them into 5 cm/2 inch lengths.

2 Thread the salmon and leeks alternately on to 8 pre-soaked wooden skewers. Leave to chill in the refrigerator until required.

3 To make the sauce, place all of the ingredients in a small pan and heat gently, stirring, until the sugar dissolves. Bring to the boil, then reduce the heat and simmer for 2 minutes. Strain the sauce and leave to cool.

4 Pour about one-third of the sauce into a small dish and set aside to serve with the kebabs (kabobs).

5 Brush plenty of the remaining sauce over the skewers and cook directly on the rack or, if preferred, place a sheet of oiled kitchen foil on the rack and cook the salmon on that. Barbecue (grill) the skewers over hot coals for about 10 minutes, turning once. Baste frequently during cooking with the remaining sauce to prevent the fish and vegetables from drying out.

6 Serve the kebabs (kabobs) with the reserved sauce for dipping.

COOK'S TIP

Soak the wooden skewers in cold water for at least 30 minutes to prevent them from burning during cooking. You can make the kebabs (kabobs) and sauce several hours before required. Keep in the refrigerator until required.

Salmon Brochettes

These tasty kebabs (kabobs) have a lovely summery flavour.
Serve on a bread croûte with fresh tomato sauce.

Serves 4

INGREDIENTS

450 g/1 lb salmon, skinned and cut
  into large chunks
1 tbsp cornflour (cornstarch)
$^1/_2$ tsp salt
$^1/_2$ tsp pepper
1 small egg white, beaten
1 red (bell) pepper, deseeded and cut
  into chunks

1 green (bell) pepper, deseeded and
  cut into chunks
4 tbsp olive oil
ciabatta bread, to serve

TOMATO SAUCE:
4 tomatoes, deseeded and quartered
$^1/_4$ cucumber, peeled, deseeded and
  chopped
8 basil leaves
6 tbsp olive oil
2 tbsp lemon juice
salt and pepper

1 Place the salmon in a shallow dish and sprinkle over the cornflour (cornstarch), and salt and pepper. Add the beaten egg white and toss well to coat. Leave to chill for 15 minutes.

2 Thread the pieces of salmon on to 4 skewers, alternating the fish pieces with the chunks of red and green (bell) peppers. Set the skewers aside while you make the tomato sauce.

3 To make the sauce, place all of the ingredients in a food processor and chop coarsely. Alternatively, chop the tomatoes, cucumber and basil leaves by hand and mix with the oil, lemon juice and seasoning. Leave to chill.

4 To serve, barbecue (grill) the salmon brochettes over hot coals for 10 minutes, brushing frequently with olive oil to prevent them from drying during cooking.

5 Slice the ciabatta bread at an angle to produce 4 long slices. Lightly toast on the barbecue (grill).

6 Spread the sauce over each slice of bread and top with a salmon brochette.

VARIATION

Serve the salmon brochettes on toasted French sticks, if preferred.

Japanese-style Char-grilled Plaice (Flounder)

The marinade for this dish has a distinctly Japanese flavour.
Its subtle flavour goes well with any white fish.

Serves 4

INGREDIENTS

4 small plaice (flounders)
6 tbsp soy sauce
2 tbsp sake or dry white wine
2 tbsp sesame oil

1 tbsp lemon juice
2 tbsp light muscovado sugar
1 tsp root (fresh) ginger, grated
1 clove garlic, crushed

TO GARNISH:
1 small carrot
4 spring onions (scallion)

1 Rinse the fish and pat them dry on absorbent kitchen paper. Cut a few slashes into both sides of each fish.

2 Mix together the soy sauce, sake or wine, oil, lemon juice, sugar, ginger and garlic in a large, shallow dish.

3 Place the fish in the marinade and turn them over so that they are well coated on both sides. Leave to stand in the refrigerator for 1–6 hours.

4 Meanwhile, prepare the garnish. Cut the carrot into evenly-sized thin sticks and clean and shred the spring onions (scallions).

5 Barbecue (grill) the fish over hot coals for about 10 minutes, turning once.

6 Scatter the chopped spring onions (scallions) and carrot over the fish and transfer the fish to a serving dish. Serve immediately.

VARIATION

Use sole instead of the plaice (flounders) and scatter over some toasted sesame seeds instead of the carrot and spring onions (scallions), if you prefer.

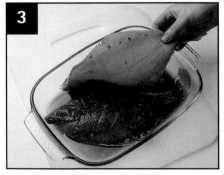

Smoky Fish Skewers

The combination of fresh and smoked fish gives these kebabs (kabobs)
a special flavour. Choose thick fish fillets to get good sized pieces.

Serves 4

INGREDIENTS

350 g/12 oz smoked cod fillet
350 g/12 oz cod fillet
8 large raw prawns (shrimp)
8 bay leaves
fresh dill, to garnish (optional)

MARINADE:
4 tbsp sunflower oil
2 tbsp lemon or lime juice
rind of 1/2 lemon or lime, grated

1/4 tsp dried dill
salt and pepper

1 Skin both types of cod and cut the flesh into bite-size pieces. Peel the prawns (shrimp), leaving just the tail.

2 To make the marinade, combine the sunflower oil, lemon or lime juice, grated lemon or lime rind, dried dill and salt and pepper to taste in a shallow, non-metallic dish.

3 Place the prepared fish in the marinade and stir together until the fish is well coated on all sides. Leave the fish to marinate for 1–4 hours.

4 Thread the fish on to 4 skewers, alternating the 2 types of cod with the prawns (shrimp) and bay leaves.

5 Cover the rack with lightly buttered kitchen foil and place the fish skewers on top of the foil.

6 Barbecue (grill) the fish skewers over hot coals for 5-10 minutes, basting with any remaining marinade, turning once.

7 Garnish with fresh dill, if using, and serve.

COOK'S TIP

Cod fillet can be rather flaky, so choose the thicker end which is easier to cut into chunky pieces. Line the rack with kitchen foil rather than cooking the fish directly on the rack so that, even if the fish does break away from the skewer, it is not wasted.

Apricot Char-grilled Mackerel

*The sharpness of the apricot glaze complements the oiliness
of the fish and has a delicious hint of ginger.*

Serves 4

INGREDIENTS

4 mackerel
400 g/14 oz can apricots
  in natural juice
3 tbsp dark muscovado sugar

3 tbsp Worcestershire sauce
3 tbsp soy sauce
2 tbsp tomato purée (paste)
1 tsp ground ginger

dash Tabasco sauce
1 clove garlic, crushed (optional)
salt and pepper

1 Clean and gut the mackerel, removing the heads if preferred. Place the fish in a shallow dish.

2 Drain the apricots, reserving the juice. Roughly chop half of the apricots and set aside.

3 Place the remaining apricots in a food processor with the sugar, Worcestershire sauce, soy sauce, tomato purée (paste), ginger, Tabasco sauce and garlic (if using) and process until smooth. Alternatively, chop the apricots and mix with the other ingredients.

4 Pour the sauce over the fish, turning them so that they are well coated on both sides. Leave to chill in the refrigerator until required.

5 Transfer the mackerel to the barbecue (grill) either directly on the rack or on a piece of greased kitchen foil. Barbecue (grill) the mackerel over hot coals for 5–7 minutes, turning once.

6 Spoon any remaining marinade into a saucepan. Add the reserved chopped apricots and about half of the reserved apricot juice and bring to the boil. Reduce the heat and simmer for 2 minutes.

7 Transfer the mackerel to a serving plate and serve with the apricot sauce.

COOK'S TIP

Use a hinged rack if you have one as it will make it much easier to turn the fish during barbecueing (grilling).

Mackerel with Lime & Coriander (Cilantro)

The secret of this dish lies in the simple, fresh flavours
which perfectly complement the fish.

Serves 4

INGREDIENTS

4 small mackerel
$^1/_4$ tsp ground coriander
$^1/_4$ tsp ground cumin
4 sprigs fresh coriander (cilantro)

3 tbsp chopped, fresh coriander (cilantro)
1 red chilli, deseeded and chopped
grated rind and juice of 1 lime

2 tbsp sunflower oil
salt and pepper
1 lime, sliced, to garnish
chilli flowers, to garnish (optional)
salad leaves, to serve

1 To make the chilli flowers (if using), cut the tip of a small chilli lengthwise into thin strips, leaving the chilli intact at the stem end. Remove the seeds and place in iced water until curled.

2 Clean and gut the mackerel, removing the heads if preferred. Transfer the mackerel to a chopping board.

3 Sprinkle the fish with the ground spices and salt and pepper to taste. Place a sprig of coriander (cilantro) inside the cavity of each fish.

4 Mix together the chopped coriander (cilantro), chilli, lime rind and juice and the oil in a small bowl. Brush the mixture liberally over the fish.

5 Place the fish in a hinged rack if you have one. Barbecue (grill) the fish over hot coals for 3–4 minutes on each side, turning once. Brush frequently with the remaining basting mixture.

6 Garnish with lime slices and chilli flowers, if using, and serve with salad leaves.

VARIATION

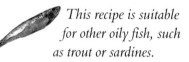

This recipe is suitable for other oily fish, such as trout or sardines.

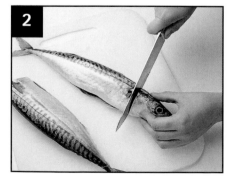

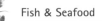

Mediterranean-style Sardines

These tasty sardines will bring back memories of Mediterranean holidays.
Serve them with crusty brown bread as a perfect starter.

Serves 4

INGREDIENTS

8–12 fresh sardines
8–12 sprigs of fresh thyme
3 tbsp lemon juice

4 tbsp olive oil
salt and pepper

TO GARNISH:
lemon wedges
tomato slices
fresh herbs

1 Clean and gut the fish if this has not already been done by the fishmonger.

2 Remove the scales from the sardines by rubbing the back of a knife from head to tail along the body. Wash and pat the sardines dry on absorbent kitchen paper.

3 Tuck a sprig of fresh thyme into the body of each sardine.

4 Transfer the sardines to a large, non-metallic dish and season with salt and pepper to taste.

5 Beat together the lemon juice and oil in a bowl and pour the mixture over the sardines. Leave the sardines to marinate in the refrigerator for about 30 minutes.

6 Remove the sardines from the marinade and place them in a hinged basket, if you have one, or on a rack. Barbecue (grill) the sardines over hot coals for 3–4 minutes on each side, basting frequently with any of the remaining marinade.

7 Serve the sardines garnished with lemon wedges, tomato slices and fresh herbs.

COOK'S TIP

Look out for small sardines or sprats. Prepare them as above and use the same marinade. Place a piece of greased kitchen foil on the rack and cook over hot coals for 2–3 minutes on each side.

VARIATION

For a slightly different flavour and texture, toss the sardines in dried breadcrumbs and then baste them with a little olive oil for a crispy coating.

Nutty Stuffed Trout

Stuff the trout just before cooking. If you prefer, the fish can be cooked in foil parcels on the barbecue.

Serves 4

INGREDIENTS

4 medium trout, cleaned
2 tbsp sunflower oil
1 small onion, chopped finely
50 g/1 3/4 oz toasted mixed nuts, chopped

rind of 1 orange, grated
2 tbsp orange juice
75 g/2 3/4 oz fresh wholemeal breadcrumbs
1 medium egg, beaten

oil for brushing
salt and pepper
orange slices, to garnish
orange and watercress salad, to serve

1 Season the trout inside and out with salt and pepper.

2 To make the stuffing, heat the oil in a small saucepan and fry the onion until soft. Remove the pan from the heat and stir in the chopped nuts, grated orange rind, orange juice and the breadcrumbs. Add just enough beaten egg to bind the mixture together.

3 Divide the stuffing into 4 equal portions and spoon into the body of each fish.

4 Brush the fish liberally with oil and barbecue (grill) over medium hot coals for 10 minutes on each side, turning once. When the fish is cooked the flesh will be white and firm and the skin will be beginning to crispen.

5 Transfer the fish to individual serving plates and garnish with orange slices.

6 Serve the fish with an orange and watercress salad and an orange and mustard dressing (see Cook's Tip, right).

COOK'S TIP

Serve the stuffed trout with an orange and watercress salad. For the dressing, mix together 2 tbsp orange juice, 1 tbsp white wine vinegar, 3 tbsp olive oil, 1/2 tsp wholegrain mustard and salt and pepper to taste. Pour the dressing over the orange and watercress salad just before serving.

Barbecued Herrings with Lemon

*Cook these fish in foil parcels for a wonderfully
moist texture. They make a perfect starter.*

Serves 4

INGREDIENTS

4 herrings, cleaned
4 bay leaves
salt

1 lemon, sliced
50 g/1³/₄ oz unsalted butter
2 tbsp chopped, fresh parsley

¹/₂ tsp lemon pepper
fresh crusty bread, to serve

1 Season the prepared herrings inside and out with freshly ground salt to taste.

2 Place a bay leaf inside the cavity of each fish.

3 Place 4 squares of kitchen foil on the work surface and divide the lemon slices evenly among them. Place a fish on top of the lemon slices.

4 Beat the butter until softened, then mix in the parsley and lemon pepper. Dot the flavoured butter liberally all over the fish.

5 Wrap the fish tightly in the kitchen foil and barbecue (grill) over medium hot coals for 15-20 minutes or until the fish is cooked through – the flesh should be white in colour and firm to the touch (unwrap the foil to check, then wrap up the fish again).

6 Transfer the wrapped fish parcels to individual, warm serving plates.

7 Unwrap the foil parcels just before serving and serve the fish with fresh, crusty bread to mop up the deliciously flavoured cooking juices.

VARIATION

For a main course use trout instead of herring. Cook for 20–30 minutes until the flesh is firm to the touch and opaque in colour.

Sardines with Olives & Tomatoes

Tomatoes flavoured with basil and olives make sardines into a tasty meal.

Serves 4

INGREDIENTS

12 fresh sardines, gutted and cleaned
fresh basil leaves
4 plum tomatoes
8 pitted black olives

15 g/¹/₂ oz butter
1 tbsp olive oil
2 tbsp lemon juice
salt and pepper

TO GARNISH:
plum tomatoes, sliced
olives, sliced
1 fresh basil sprig

1 Season the sardines inside and out with salt and pepper to taste. Insert 1-2 basil leaves inside the cavity of each fish. Using a sharp knife, make a few slashes in the body of each fish.

2 Cut the tomatoes and olives into slices and transfer to a large bowl. Tear 4 basil leaves into small pieces and toss together with the tomatoes and olives.

3 Divide the tomato and olive mixture among 4 large sheets of kitchen foil, and place 3 sardines on top of each portion.

4 Melt the butter and oil together in a small pan. Stir in the lemon juice and pour the mixture over the fish.

5 Carefully wrap up the fish in the foil. Barbecue (grill) the fish over medium hot coals for 15–20 minutes until the fish is firm and cooked through.

6 Transfer the fish to individual serving plates and remove the kitchen foil. Garnish the fish with slices of tomato and olive, and with a fresh sprig of basil. Serve at once.

COOK'S TIP

Slashing the body of the fish helps the flesh to absorb the flavours. It is particularly important if you do not have time to allow the fish to marinate before cooking.

VARIATION

You can barbecue (grill) trout or mackerel in exactly the same way as the sardines but remember to increase the cooking time to 20–30 minutes.

Bacon & Scallop Skewers

Wrapping bacon around the scallops helps to protect the delicate flesh from the intense heat and allows them to cook without becoming tough. The bacon also imparts a subtle smoky flavour to the scallops.

Makes 4

INGREDIENTS

grated rind and juice of $\frac{1}{2}$ lemon	12 scallops	1 yellow (bell) pepper
4 tbsp sunflower oil	1 red (bell) pepper	6 rashers smoked streaky bacon
$\frac{1}{2}$ tsp dried dill	1 green (bell) pepper	

1 Mix together the lemon rind and juice, oil and dill in a non-metallic dish. Add the scallops and mix thoroughly to coat in the marinade. Leave to marinate for 1–2 hours.

2 Cut the red, green and yellow (bell) peppers in half and deseed them. Cut the (bell) pepper halves into 2.5 cm/1 inch pieces and then set aside until required.

3 Carefully remove the rind from the bacon. Stretch the bacon rashers with the back of a knife, then cut each bacon rasher in half.

4 Remove the scallops from the marinade, reserving any excess marinade. Wrap a piece of bacon around each scallop.

5 Thread the bacon-wrapped scallops on to skewers, alternating with the (bell) pepper pieces.

6 Barbecue (grill) the bacon and scallop skewers over hot coals for about 5 minutes, basting frequently with the lemon and oil marinade.

7 Transfer the bacon and scallop skewers to serving plates and serve at once.

VARIATION

Peel 4–8 raw prawns (shrimp) and add them to the marinade with the scallops. Thread them on to the skewers alternately with the scallops and (bell) peppers.

COOK'S TIP

Hold the skewers with oven gloves (potholders) when you are turning them on the barbecue (grill).

Herrings with Orange Tarragon Stuffing

*The fish are filled with an orange-flavoured stuffing and are wrapped
in kitchen foil before being baked on the barbecue (grill).*

Serves 4

INGREDIENTS

1 orange
4 spring onions (scallions)
50 g/1³/₄ oz fresh wholemeal
   breadcrumbs
1 tbsp fresh tarragon, chopped

4 herrings, cleaned and gutted
salt and pepper
green salad, to serve

TO GARNISH:
2 oranges
1 tbsp light brown sugar
1 tbsp olive oil
sprigs of fresh tarragon

1 To make the stuffing, grate the rind from half of the orange, using a zester.

2 Peel and chop all of the orange flesh on a plate in order to catch all of the juice.

3 Mix together the orange flesh, juice, rind, spring onions (scallions), breadcrumbs and tarragon in a bowl. Season with salt and pepper to taste.

4 Divide the stuffing into 4 equal portions and use it to fill the body cavities of the fish.

5 Place each fish on to a square of lightly greased kitchen foil and wrap the foil around the fish so that it is completely enclosed. Barbecue (grill) over hot coals for 20–30 minutes until the fish are cooked through – the flesh should be white and firm to the touch.

6 Meanwhile make the garnish. Peel and thickly slice the 2 oranges and sprinkle over the sugar. Just before the fish is cooked, drizzle a little oil over the orange slices and place them on the barbecue for about 5 minutes to heat through.

7 Transfer the fish to serving plates and garnish with the barbecued (grilled) orange slices and sprigs of fresh tarragon. Serve with a green salad.

VARIATION

Use any oily fish for this dish - trout and mackerel are ideal. In addition. try lemons instead of oranges for a different citrusy flavour.

Caribbean Prawns (Shrimp)

*This is an ideal recipe for cooks who have difficulty
in finding raw prawns (shrimp).*

Serves 4

INGREDIENTS

16 cooked king (tiger) prawns
(shrimp)
1 small pineapple
flaked coconut, to garnish (optional)

MARINADE:
150 ml/5 fl oz/²/₃ cup pineapple juice
2 tbsp white wine vinegar

2 tbsp dark muscovado sugar
2 tbsp desiccated (shredded) coconut

1 If they are unpeeled, peel the prawns (shrimp), leaving the tails attached if preferred.

2 Peel the pineapple and cut it in half lengthwise. Cut one pineapple half into wedges then into chunks.

3 To make the marinade, mix together half of the pineapple juice and the vinegar, sugar and coconut in a shallow, non-metallic dish. Add the peeled prawns (shrimp) and pineapple chunks and toss until well coated. Leave the prawns and pineapple to marinate for at least 30 minutes.

4 Remove the pineapple and prawns (shrimp) from the marinade and thread them on to skewers. Reserve the marinade.

5 Strain the marinade and place in a food processor. Roughly chop the remaining pineapple and add to the processor with the remaining pineapple juice. Process the pineapple for a few seconds to produce a thick sauce.

6 Pour the sauce into a small saucepan. Bring to the boil then simmer for about 5 minutes. This can be done by the side of the barbecue (grill), if preferred.

7 Transfer the kebabs (kabobs) to the barbecue (grill) and brush with some of the sauce. Barbecue (grill) for about 5 minutes until the kebabs (kabobs) are piping hot. Turn the kebabs (kabobs), brushing occasionally with the sauce. Serve with extra sauce, sprinkled with flaked coconut (if using), on the side.

COOK'S TIP

*Barbecue (grill) these kebabs
(kabobs) just long enough to heat
thorough. If cooked for too long the
prawns (shrimp) will toughen.*

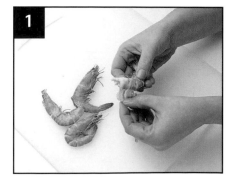

Herb & Garlic Prawns (Shrimp)

*Look for raw prawns (shrimp) in the freezer compartment
of large supermarkets or oriental food stores.*

Serves 4

INGREDIENTS

350 g/12 oz raw prawns
  (shrimp), peeled
2 tbsp chopped, fresh parsley

4 tbsp lemon juice
2 tbsp olive oil
65 g/2¼ oz butter

2 cloves garlic, chopped
salt and pepper

1 Place the prepared prawns
(shrimp) in a shallow, non-metallic dish with the parsley, lemon juice and salt and pepper to taste. Leave the prawns (shrimp) to marinate in the herb mixture for at least 30 minutes.

2 Heat the oil and butter in a small pan with the garlic until the butter melts. Stir to mix thoroughly.

3 Remove the prawns (shrimp) from the marinade with a perforated spoon and add them to the pan containing the garlic butter. Stir the prawns (shrimp)

into the garlic butter until well coated, then thread the prawns (shrimp) on to skewers.

4 Barbecue (grill) the kebabs (kabobs) over hot coals for 5–10 minutes, turning the skewers occasionally, until the prawns (shrimp) turn pink and are cooked through. Brush the prawns (shrimp) with the remaining garlic butter during the cooking time.

5 Transfer the herb and garlic prawn (shrimp) kebabs (kabobs) to serving plates. Drizzle over any of the remaining garlic butter and serve at once.

VARIATION

If raw prawns (shrimp) are unavailable, use cooked prawns (shrimp) but reduce the cooking time. Small cooked prawns (shrimp) can also be cooked in a kitchen foil parcel istead of on the skewers. Marinate and toss the cooked prawns (shrimp) in the garlic butter, wrap in a kitchen foil and cook for about 5 minutes, shaking the parcels once or twice.

Poultry

Poultry is a versatile food that can be cooked in a number of ways on the barbecue (grill). Try it with herbs and garlic, tangy tomato glazes or spicy oriental flavours. It also goes well with sweet glazes and fruit.

Chicken is ideal for the barbecue because the skin helps to keep the flesh succulent and gives a crispy coating. It is, however, essential that all poultry is cooked thoroughly. Test by piercing with a skewer in the thickest part – the juices should run clear when the meat is cooked. To avoid charred skins and raw centres, cook over coals that are not too hot. Place the rack about 10 cm/4 inches above the coals. You should be able to hold your hand just above the rack for about 5 seconds; if it is too hot reduce the temperature by raising the rack or spreading out the coals. However if the coals are not hot enough, the chicken will take too long to cook and will dry out.

Turkey can be a little dry, so baste it frequently with a glaze or marinade. Duckling has a stronger flavour and more fat than chicken or turkey, and it stands up very well to the barbecue (grill) treatment. Larger joints of poultry can be par-cooked in boiling water, the oven or microwave and finished on the barbecue (grill).

Jerk Chicken

This is perhaps one of the best known Caribbean dishes. The 'jerk' in the name refers to the hot spicy coating.

Serves 4

INGREDIENTS

4 chicken portions
1 bunch spring onions (scallions), trimmed
1–2 Scotch Bonnet chillies, deseeded
1 garlic clove

5 cm/2 inch piece root (fresh) ginger, peeled and roughly chopped
1/2 tsp dried thyme
1/2 tsp paprika
1/4 tsp ground allspice

pinch ground cinnamon
pinch ground cloves
4 tbsp white wine vinegar
3 tbsp light soy sauce
pepper

1 Rinse the chicken portions and pat them dry on absorbent kitchen paper. Place them in a shallow dish.

2 Place the spring onions (scallions), chillies, garlic, ginger, thyme, paprika, allspice, cinnamon, cloves, wine vinegar, soy sauce and pepper to taste in a food processor and process to make a smooth mixture.

3 Pour the spicy mixture over the chicken. Turn the chicken portions over so that they are well coated in the marinade. Transfer the chicken to the refrigerator and leave to marinate for up to 24 hours.

4 Remove the chicken from the marinade and barbecue (grill) over medium hot coals for about 30 minutes, turning the chicken over and basting occasionally with any remaining marinade, until the chicken is cooked through.

5 Transfer the chicken portions to individual serving plates and serve at once.

COOK'S TIP

As Jamaican cuisine becomes increasingly popular, you will find jars of ready-made jerk marinade, which you can use when time is short. Allow the chicken to marinate for as long as possible for maximum flavour.

VARIATION

You can use milder chillies or even increase the amount of chilli used.

Favourite Barbecued (Grilled) Chicken

These chicken wings are brushed with a simple barbecue (grill) glaze, which can be made in minutes, but the results are sure to delight everyone.

Serves 4

INGREDIENTS

8 chicken wings or 1 chicken cut into
   8 portions
3 tbsp tomato purée (paste)

3 tbsp brown fruity sauce
1 tbsp white wine vinegar
1 tbsp clear honey

1 tbsp olive oil
1 clove garlic, crushed (optional)
salad leaves, to serve

1 Remove the skin from the chicken if you want to reduce the fat in the dish.

2 To make the barbecue glaze, place the tomato purée (paste), brown fruity sauce, white wine vinegar, honey, oil and garlic in a small bowl. Stir all of the ingredients together until they are thoroughly blended.

3 Brush the barbecue (grill) glaze over the chicken and barbecue (grill) over hot coals for 15–20 minutes. Turn the chicken portions over occasionally and baste frequently with the barbecue (grill) glaze. If the chicken begins to blacken before it is cooked, raise the rack if possible or move the chicken to a cooler part of the barbecue (grill) to slow down the cooking.

4 Transfer the barbecued (grilled) chicken to warm serving plates and serve with fresh salad leaves.

VARIATION

This barbecue (grill) glaze also makes a very good baste to brush over pork chops.

COOK'S TIP

When poultry is cooked over a very hot barbecue (grill) the heat immediately seals in all of the juices, leaving the meat succulent. For this reason you must make sure that the coals are hot enough before starting to barbecue (grill).

Sticky Chicken Drumsticks

These drumsticks are always popular with children - make sure there are plenty of napkins for wiping sticky fingers or provide finger bowls with a slice of lemon.

Serves 10

INGREDIENTS

10 chicken drumsticks
4 tbsp fine-cut orange marmalade

1 tbsp Worcestershire sauce
grated rind and juice of $^1/_2$ orange
salt and pepper

TO SERVE:
cherry tomatoes
salad leaves

1 Using a sharp knife, make 2–3 slashes in the flesh of each chicken drumstick.

2 Bring a large saucepan of water to the boil and add the chicken drumsticks. Cover the pan, return to the boil and cook for 5–10 minutes. Remove the chicken and drain thoroughly.

3 Meanwhile, make the baste. Place the orange marmalade, Worcestershire sauce, orange rind and juice and salt and pepper to taste in a small saucepan. Heat gently, stirring continuously, until the marmalade melts and all of the ingredients are well combined.

4 Brush the baste over the par-cooked chicken drumsticks and transfer them to the barbecue (grill) to complete cooking. Barbecue (grill) over hot coals for about 10 minutes, turning and basting frequently with the remaining baste.

5 Carefully thread 3 cherry tomatoes on to a skewer and transfer to the barbecue (grill) for 1–2 minutes.

6 Transfer the chicken drumsticks to serving plates. Serve with the cherry tomato skewers and a selection of fresh salad leaves.

COOK'S TIP

Par-cooking the chicken is an ideal way of making sure that it is cooked through without becoming overcooked and burned on the outside.

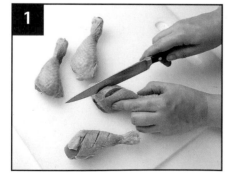

Chicken Tikka

*Traditionally, chicken tikka is cooked in a clay tandoori
oven, but it works well on the barbecue (grill) too.*

Makes 6

INGREDIENTS

4 chicken breasts, skinned and boned
$^1/_2$ tsp salt
4 tbsp lemon or lime juice

MARINADE:
150 ml/5 fl oz /$^2/_3$ cup natural yogurt
2 cloves garlic, crushed

2.5 cm/1 inch piece root (fresh)
  ginger, peeled and grated
1 tsp ground cumin
1 tsp chilli powder
$^1/_2$ tsp ground coriander
$^1/_2$ tsp ground turmeric
oil or melted butter for brushing

SAUCE:
150 ml/5 fl oz/ $^2/_3$ cup natural yogurt
1 tsp mint sauce

1 Cut the chicken into 2.5 cm/ 1 inch cubes. Sprinkle with the salt and the lemon or lime juice and leave to stand for about 10 minutes.

2 To make the marinade, combine the yogurt, garlic, ginger and ground spices together in a small bowl until well mixed.

3 Thread the cubes of chicken on to skewers. Brush the marinade over the chicken. Cover and leave to marinate in the refrigerator for at least 2 hours, preferably overnight.

4 Barbecue (grill) the chicken skewers over hot coals, brushing with oil or butter and turning frequently, for about 15 minutes or until cooked through.

5 Meanwhile, combine the yogurt and mint to make the sauce. Serve the chicken skewers with the mint and yogurt sauce.

VARIATION

Use the marinade to coat chicken portions, such as drumsticks, rather than cubes of chicken, if you prefer. Barbecue (grill) over medium hot coals for 30–40 minutes, until the juices run clear when the chicken is pierced with a skewer.

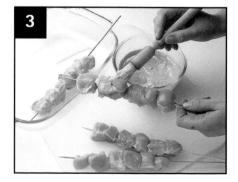

Indian Charred Chicken

*An Indian-influenced dish that is delicious served
with naan bread and a cucumber raita.*

Serves 4

INGREDIENTS

4 chicken breasts, skinned and boned
2 tbsp curry paste
1 tbsp sunflower oil
1 tbsp light muscovado sugar
1 tsp ground ginger
$^1/_2$ tsp ground cumin

TO SERVE:
naan bread
green salad leaves

CUCUMBER RAITA:
$^1/_4$ cucumber
salt
150 ml/5 fl oz/ $^2/_3$ cup natural yogurt
$^1/_4$ tsp chilli powder

1 Place the chicken breasts between 2 sheets of baking parchment or cling film (plastic wrap). Pound them with the flat side of a meat mallet or rolling pin to flatten them.

2 Mix together the curry paste, oil, sugar, ginger and cumin in a small bowl. Spread the mixture over both sides of the chicken and set aside until required.

3 To make the raita, peel the cucumber and scoop out the seeds with a spoon. Grate the cucumber flesh, sprinkle with salt, place in a sieve and leave to stand for 10 minutes. Rinse off the salt and squeeze out any moisture by pressing the cucumber with the base of a glass or back of a spoon.

4 To make the raita, mix the cucumber with the yogurt and stir in the chilli powder. Leave to chill until required.

5 Transfer the chicken to an oiled rack and barbecue (grill) over hot coals for 10 minutes, turning once.

6 Warm the naan bread at the side of the barbecue. Serve the chicken with the naan bread and raita and accompanied with fresh green salad leaves.

COOK'S TIP

*Flattening the chicken breasts
makes them thinner so that they
cook more quickly.*

Cajun Spicy Chicken

The Cajun spices are rubbed into the chicken, which is left to stand so that the flavours have time to penetrate the flesh and develop.

Serves 4

INGREDIENTS

4 chicken portions
1 clove garlic
1 tbsp light muscovado sugar
3 tbsp paprika

2 tsp cayenne pepper
1 tsp dried oregano
1 tsp dried sage
1 tsp dried thyme

4 tbsp sunflower oil
2 tbsp lemon juice
salt and pepper

1 Remove the skin from the chicken if you want to reduce the fat content of this recipe. Using a sharp knife, make 2–3 slashes in the flesh of the chicken.

2 Cut the garlic clove in half and rub the cut surface over the chicken. Season the chicken portions with salt and pepper to taste.

3 Mix together the sugar, spices and dried herbs in a small bowl. Sprinkle over the chicken and rub into the flesh. Cover and leave to stand for at least 2 hours.

4 Mix together the oil and lemon juice in a small bowl. Brush the mixture liberally over the chicken.

5 Barbecue (grill) the chicken over medium hot coals for about 30 minutes, turning and basting occasionally with the oil and lemon mixture.

6 Check that the chicken is cooked by piercing the thickest part with a skewer – the juices should run clear. Return the chicken to the barbecue (grill) to cook for a little longer if necessary.

7 Transfer the chicken to warm serving plates and serve at once.

VARIATION

This recipe also works well with pork. Rub the spiced mixture on to pork chops or belly pork slices – they will taste delicious.

Spatchcock Baby Chicken with Garlic & Herbs

It is not difficult to spatchcock (open out) baby chickens, but it is the best way to cook whole birds on the barbecue (grill).

Serves 2

INGREDIENTS

2 baby chickens, each 450 g/1lb	BASTE:	salt and pepper
75 g/2³/₄ oz butter	4 tbsp olive oil	
2 cloves garlic, crushed	2 tbsp lemon juice	
2 tbsp chopped, mixed fresh herbs	2 tbsp chopped, mixed herbs	

1 To spatchcock each chicken, place each bird on its breast and use sharp scissors or poultry shears to cut along the length of the back bone. Open out the bird as much as possible and place it breast-side up on a chopping board. Press down firmly on the breast bone to break it.

2 Mix together the butter, garlic and herbs until well combined. Lift up the skin from the breast of each chicken. Divide the butter equally between the 2 chickens and spread over the breast under the skin.

3 Open out each bird. Thread 2 skewers diagonally through each bird to hold it flat.

4 Mix together the ingredients for the baste in a bowl.

5 Place the birds, bone-side down, over medium hot coals and barbecue (grill) for 25 minutes, basting with the lemon and herb baste. Turn the birds over and barbecue (grill), skin-side down, for 15 minutes, basting frequently, or until cooked through.

COOK'S TIP

Use a combination of whatever fresh herbs you have to hand. Thyme, rosemary, mint, oregano, parsley or coriander (cilantro) are all suitable. If you want to cook a whole chicken in this way double the amount of baste and cook for 40–50 minutes.

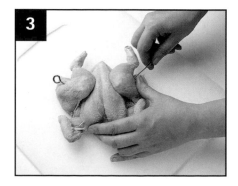

Sweet Maple Chicken

You can use any chicken portions for this recipe. Boned chicken thighs are economical for large barbecue (grill) parties, but you could also use wings or drumsticks.

Serves 6

INGREDIENTS

2 boned chicken thighs
5 tbsp maple syrup
1 tbsp caster (superfine) sugar
grated rind and juice of $1/2$ orange
2 tbsp tomato ketchup (catsup)

2 tsp Worcestershire sauce

TO GARNISH:
slices of orange
sprig of flat-leaf parsley

TO SERVE:
focaccia bread
salad leaves
cherry tomatoes, quartered

1 Using a sharp knife, make 2–3 slashes in the flesh of the chicken. Place the chicken in a shallow, non-metallic dish.

2 To make the marinade, mix together the maple syrup, sugar, orange rind and juice, ketchup and Worcestershire sauce in a small bowl.

3 Pour the marinade over the chicken, tossing the chicken to coat thoroughly. Cover and leave to chill in the refrigerator until required.

4 Remove the chicken from the marinade, reserving the marinade for basting.

5 Transfer the chicken to the barbecue (grill) and cook over hot coals for 20 minutes, turning the chicken and basting with the marinade frequently.

6 Transfer the chicken to serving plates and garnish with slices of orange and a sprig of fresh-leaf parsley. Serve with focaccia bread, fresh salad leaves and cherry tomatoes.

COOK'S TIP

If time is short you can omit the marinating time. If you use chicken quarters, rather than the smaller thigh portions, par-boil them for 10 minutes before brushing with the marinade and barbecueing (grilling).

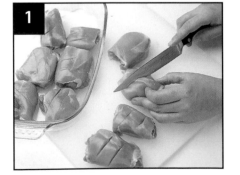

Chicken Skewers with Lemon & Coriander (Cilantro)

A tangy lemon yogurt is served with this tasty chicken dish.

Serves 4

INGREDIENTS

4 chicken breasts, skinned and boned
1 tsp ground coriander
2 tsp lemon juice

300 ml/ ^{1}/$_2$ pint/1 ^{1}/$_4$ cups natural
   yogurt
1 lemon

2 tbsp chopped, fresh coriander
   (cilantro)
oil for brushing
salt and pepper

1 Cut the chicken into 2.5 cm/ 1 inch pieces and place them in a shallow, non-metallic dish.

2 Add the coriander, lemon juice, salt and pepper to taste and 4 tbsp of the yogurt to the chicken and mix together until thoroughly combined. Cover and leave to chill for at least 2 hours, preferably overnight.

3 To make the lemon yogurt, peel and finely chop the lemon, discarding any pips. Stir the lemon into the yogurt together with the fresh coriander (cilantro). Leave to chill in the refrigerator until required.

4 Thread the chicken pieces on to skewers. Brush the rack with oil and barbecue (grill) the chicken over hot coals for about 15 minutes, basting with the oil.

5 Transfer the chicken kebabs (kabobs) to warm serving plates and garnish with a sprig of fresh coriander (cilantro), lemon wedges and fresh salad leaves. Serve with the lemon yogurt.

VARIATION

 These kebabs (kabobs) are delicious served on a bed of blanched spinach, which has been seasoned with salt, pepper and nutmeg.

COOK'S TIP

Prepare the chicken the day before it is needed so that it can marinate overnight. This will allow the flavours to be fully absorbed.

Chicken Satay

*This is an ideal sauce to accompany food cooked on the barbecue (grill),
and it can be kept warm at the side of the rack.*

Serves 4

INGREDIENTS

2 chicken breasts, skinned and boned

MARINADE:
4 tbsp sunflower oil
2 cloves garlic, crushed
3 tbsp fresh, chopped coriander
   (cilantro)
1 tbsp caster (superfine) sugar

$^1/_2$ tsp ground cumin
$^1/_2$ tsp ground coriander
1 tbsp soy sauce
1 red or green chilli, deseeded
salt and pepper

SAUCE:
2 tbsp sunflower oil

1 small onion, chopped finely
1 red or green chilli, deseeded and
   chopped
$^1/_2$ tsp ground coriander
$^1/_2$ tsp ground cumin
8 tbsp peanut butter
8 tbsp chicken stock or water
1 tbsp block coconut

1 Soak 8 wooden skewers in a large, shallow dish of cold water for at least 30 minutes. This process will prevent the skewers from burning during barbecueing (grilling).

2 Cut the chicken lengthwise into 8 long strips. Thread the strips of chicken, concertina-style, on to the skewers and set aside while you make the marinade.

3 Place the ingredients for the marinade in a food processor and process until smooth.

4 Coat the chicken with the marinade paste, cover and leave to chill in the refrigerator for at least 2 hours.

5 To make the sauce, heat the oil in a small pan and fry the onion and chilli until they are

softened but not browned. Stir in the spices and cook for 1 minute. Add the remaining sauce ingredients and cook the mixture gently for 5 minutes. Keep warm at the side of the barbecue (grill).

6 Barbecue (grill) the chicken skewers over hot coals for about 10 minutes, basting with any remaining marinade. Serve with the warm sauce.

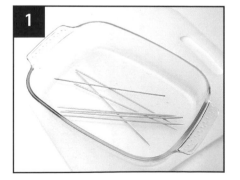

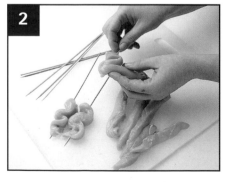

Thai-style Chicken Skewers

Here the chicken is marinated in a delicious aromatic sauce
before being threaded on to skewers.

Serves 4

INGREDIENTS

4 chicken breasts, skinned and boned
1 onion, peeled and cut into wedges
1 large red (bell) pepper, deseeded
1 large yellow (bell) pepper deseeded

12 kaffir lime leaves
2 tbsp sunflower oil
2 tbsp lime juice
tomato halves, to serve

MARINADE:
1 tbsp Thai red curry paste
150 ml/5 fl oz/^{2}/3 cup canned
  coconut milk

1 To make the marinade, place the red curry paste in a small pan over medium heat and cook for 1 minute. Add half of the coconut milk to the pan and bring the mixture to the boil. Boil for 2–3 minutes until the liquid has reduced by about two-thirds.

2 Remove the pan from the heat and stir in the remaining coconut milk. Set aside to cool.

3 Cut the chicken into 2.5 cm/ 1 inch pieces. Stir the chicken into the cold marinade, cover and leave to chill for at least 2 hours.

4 Cut the onion into wedges and the (bell) peppers into 2.5 cm/1 inch pieces.

5 Remove the chicken pieces from the marinade and thread them on to skewers, alternating the chicken with the vegetables and lime leaves.

6 Combine the oil and lime juice in a small bowl and brush the mixture over the kebabs (kabobs). Barbecue (grill) the skewers over hot coals, turning and basting frequently for 10–15 minutes until the chicken is

cooked through. Barbecue (grill) the tomato halves and serve with the chicken skewers.

COOK'S TIP

Cooking the marinade first intensifies the flavour. It is important to allow the marinade to cool before adding the chicken, or bacteria may breed in the warm temperature. You will find fresh kaffir lime leaves in oriental stores, but if these are unavailable bay leaves can be used instead.

Sesame Chicken Brochettes with Cranberry Sauce

The cranberries give the sauce a lovely tart flavour. It can be served hot or cold.

Makes 8

INGREDIENTS

4 chicken breasts, skinned and boned
4 tbsp dry white wine
1 tbsp light muscovado sugar
2 tbsp sunflower oil
100 g/3¹/₂ oz sesame seeds
salt and pepper

TO SERVE:
boiled new potatoes
green salad leaves

SAUCE:
175 g/6 oz cranberries
150 ml/5 fl oz/²/₃ cup cranberry juice
  drink
2 tbsp light muscovado sugar

1 Cut the chicken into 2.5 cm/ 1 inch pieces. Put the wine, sugar, oil and salt and pepper to taste in a large bowl, stirring to combine. Add the chicken pieces and toss to coat. Leave to marinate for at least 30 minutes, turning the chicken occasionally.

2 To make the sauce, place the ingredients in a small saucepan and bring slowly to the boil, stirring. Simmer gently for 5–10 minutes until the cranberries are soft and pulpy. Taste and add a little extra sugar if wished. Keep warm or leave to chill as required.

3 Remove the chicken pieces from the marinade with a perforated spoon. Thread the chicken pieces on to 8 skewers, spacing them slightly apart to ensure even cooking.

4 Barbecue (grill) on an oiled rack over hot coals for 4–5 minutes on each side until just cooked. Brush several times with the marinade during cooking.

5 Remove the chicken skewers from the rack and roll in the sesame seeds. Return to the barbecue (grill) and cook for about 1 minute on each side or until the sesame seeds are toasted.Serve with the cranberry sauce, new potatoes and green salad leaves.

VARIATION

Cranberry sauce goes well with all types of poultry. Try it with turkey or guinea fowl.

Chicken Skewers with Red (Bell) Pepper Sauce

These kebabs (kabobs) are rather special and are well worth the extra effort needed to prepare them.

Serves 4

INGREDIENTS

3 chicken breasts, skinned and boned
6 tbsp olive oil
4 tbsp lemon juice
1/2 small onion, grated
1 tbsp fresh, chopped sage
8 tbsp sage and onion stuffing mix

6 tbsp boiling water
2 green (bell) peppers, deseeded

SAUCE:
1 tbsp olive oil
1 red (bell) pepper, deseeded and

chopped finely
1 small onion, chopped finely
pinch sugar
210 g/7 1/2 oz can chopped tomatoes

1 Cut the chicken into evenly sized pieces.

2 Mix the oil, lemon juice, grated onion and sage and pour the mixture into a polythene (plastic) bag. Add the chicken, seal the bag and shake to coat the chicken. Leave to marinate for at least 30 minutes, shaking the bag occasionally.

3 Place the stuffing mix in a bowl and add the boiling water, stirring to mix well.

4 Cut each (bell) pepper into 6 strips, then blanch them in boiling water for 3–4 minutes until softened. Drain and refresh under running water, then drain again.

5 Form about 1 teaspoon of the stuffing mixture into a ball and roll it up in a strip of (bell) pepper. Repeat for the remaining stuffing mixture and (bell) pepper strips. Thread 3 (bell) pepper rolls on to each skewer alternately with pieces of chicken. Leave to chill.

6 To make the sauce, heat the oil in a small pan and fry the red (bell) pepper and onion for 5 minutes. Add the sugar and tomatoes and simmer for about 5 minutes. Set aside and keep warm.

7 Barbecue (grill) the skewers on an oiled rack over hot coals, basting frequently with the remaining marinade, for about 15 minutes until the chicken is cooked. Serve with the red (bell) pepper sauce.

Maryland Chicken Kebabs (Kabobs)

A barbecue (grill) variation of the traditional dish,
Chicken Maryland. Serve with corn-on-the-cob (see page 198).

Makes 4

INGREDIENTS

8 chicken thighs, skinned and boned
1 tbsp white wine vinegar
1 tbsp lemon juice
1 tbsp golden syrup or clear honey
6 tbsp olive oil

1 clove garlic, crushed
4 rashers rindless, smoked, streaky
  bacon
2 bananas
salt and pepper

TO SERVE:
4 cooked sweetcorn (see page 198)
mango chutney (relish)

1 Cut the chicken into bite-size pieces. Combine the vinegar, lemon juice, syrup or honey, oil, garlic and salt and pepper to taste in a large bowl. Add the chicken to the marinade and toss until the chicken is well coated. Cover and leave to marinate for 1-2 hours.

2 Stretch the bacon rashers with the back of a knife and then cut each bacon rasher in half. Cut the bananas into 2.5 cm/ 1 inch lengths and brush them with lemon juice to prevent any discoloration.

3 Wrap a piece of bacon around each piece of banana.

4 Remove the chicken from the marinade, reserving the marinade for basting. Thread the chicken pieces and the bacon and banana rolls alternately on to skewers.

5 Barbecue (grill) the kebabs (kabobs) over hot coals for 8–10 minutes until the chicken is completely cooked. Baste the kebabs (kabobs) with the marinade and turn the skewers frequently.

6 Serve with corn-on-the-cob and mango chutney (relish).

VARIATION

For a quick Maryland-style dish, omit the marinating time and cook the chicken thighs over hot coals for about 20 minutes, basting with the marinade. Barbecue (grill) the bananas in their skins alongside the chicken. Serve the bananas split open with a teaspoon of mango chutney (relish).

Turkey Steaks with Redcurrant Glaze

Prepare these steaks the day before they are needed and serve in toasted ciabatta bread accompanied with crisp salad leaves.

Serves 4

INGREDIENTS

100 g/ 3^1/$_2$ oz redcurrant jelly
2 tbsp lime juice
4 tbsp olive oil
2 tbsp dry white wine

^{1}/$_4$ tsp ground ginger
pinch grated nutmeg
4 turkey breast steaks
salt and pepper

TO SERVE:
mixed salad leaves
vinaigrette dressing
1 ciabatta loaf
cherry tomatoes

1 Put the redcurrant jelly and lime juice in a small pan and heat gently, stirring, until the jelly melts. Stir in the oil, wine, ginger and nutmeg.

2 Place the turkey steaks in a shallow, non-metallic dish and season with salt and pepper. Pour over the redcurrant mixture, turning the meat so that it is well coated. Cover and leave to chill in the refrigerator overnight.

3 Remove the turkey from the marinade, reserving the marinade for basting, and barbecue (grill) on an oiled rack over hot coals for about 4 minutes on each side. Baste the turkey steaks frequently with the reserved marinade.

4 Meanwhile, toss the salad leaves in the vinaigrette dressing. Cut the ciabatta loaf in half lengthwise and place, cut-side down, at the side of the barbecue. Barbecue (grill) until golden.

5 Cut each piece of bread into 4. Serve the turkey steaks on top of a salad leaf and sandwiched between 2 pieces of bread.

VARIATION

Turkey and chicken escalopes are also ideal for cooking on the barbecue (grill). Because they are thin, they cook through without burning on the outside. Leave them overnight in a marinade of your choice or cook, basting with a little lemon juice and oil mixture, and season well.

Char-grilled Turkey with Cheesy Pockets

Wrapping bacon around the turkey helps to keep the cheese enclosed in the pocket.

Serves 4

INGREDIENTS

4 turkey breast pieces, each about 225 g/8 oz

4 portions full-fat cheese (such as Bel Paese), 15 g/^{1}/$_2$ oz each

4 sage leaves or ^{1}/$_2$ tsp dried sage

8 rashers rindless streaky bacon

4 tbsp olive oil

2 tbsp lemon juice

salt and pepper

TO SERVE:

garlic bread

salad leaves

cherry tomatoes

1 Carefully cut a pocket into the side of each turkey breast. Open out each breast a little and season inside with salt and pepper to taste.

2 Place a portion of cheese into each pocket, spreading it a little with a knife. Tuck a sage leaf into each pocket, or sprinkle with a little dried sage if you prefer.

3 Stretch the bacon out with the back of a knife. Wrap 2 pieces of bacon around each turkey breast, so that the pocket opening is completely covered.

4 Mix together the oil and lemon juice in a small bowl.

5 Barbecue (grill) the turkey over medium hot coals for about 10 minutes on each side, basting with the oil and lemon mixture frequently.

6 Place the garlic bread at the side of the barbecue (grill) and toast lightly.

7 Transfer the turkey to warm serving plates. Serve with the toasted garlic bread, salad leaves and a few cherry tomatoes.

VARIATION

You can vary the cheese you use to stuff the turkey – try grated Mozzarella or slices of Brie or Camembert. Also try placing 1 teaspoon of redcurrant jelly or cranberry sauce into each pocket instead of the sage.

COOK'S TIP

If you wish, use a cocktail stick (toothpick) to keep the turkey and bacon in place while they cook.

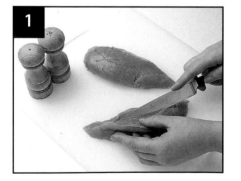

Spicy Turkey & Sausage Kebabs (Kabobs)

Serve these tasty kebabs (kabobs) with fresh bread such as ciabatta, focaccia or a French stick.

Makes 8

INGREDIENTS

turkey breast fillet, about 350 g/12 oz
300 g/10 $\frac{1}{2}$ oz chorizo (seasoned
  pork) sausage
1 dessert (eating) apple
1 tbsp lemon juice
8 bay leaves

BASTE:
6 tbsp olive oil
2 cloves garlic, crushed
1 red chilli, deseeded and chopped
salt and pepper

1 To make the baste, place the oil, garlic, chilli and salt and pepper to taste in a small screw-top jar and shake well to combine. Leave to stand for 1 hour for the garlic and chilli to flavour the oil.

2 Cut the turkey into 2.5 cm/ 1 inch pieces. Cut the sausage into 2.5 cm/1 inch lengths.

3 Cut the apple into chunks and remove the core. Toss the apple in lemon juice to prevent discoloration.

4 Thread the turkey and sausage pieces on to 8 skewers, alternating with the apple chunks and bay leaves.

5 Barbecue (grill) the kebabs (kabobs) over hot coals for about 15 minutes or until the turkey is cooked. Turn and baste the kebabs (kabobs) frequently with the flavoured oil.

6 Transfer the kebabs (kabobs) to warm serving plates and serve at once.

COOK'S TIP

The flavoured oil used in this recipe can be used to baste any grilled (broiled) meat, fish or vegetables. It will give plain foods a subtle chilli flavour and will keep in the refrigerator for about 2 weeks.

Sherried Chicken Liver Brochettes

Economical and flavoursome, these tasty kebabs
(kabobs) make an ideal light lunch

Serves 4

INGREDIENTS

400 g/14 oz chicken liver, trimmed
  and cleaned
3 slices rindless, streaky bacon
1 ciabatta loaf or small French stick
225 g/8 oz baby spinach, washed

MARINADE:
150 ml/5 fl oz/^{2}/$_3$ cup dry sherry
4 tbsp olive oil
1 tsp wholegrain mustard
salt and pepper

MUSTARD MAYONNAISE:
8 tbsp mayonnaise
1 tsp wholegrain mustard

1 Cut the chicken liver into 5 cm/2 inch pieces. To make the marinade, combine the sherry, oil, mustard and salt and pepper to taste in a shallow dish. Add the chicken liver to the marinade and toss until well coated. Leave to marinate for 3–4 hours.

2 To make the mayonnaise, stir the mustard into the mayonnaise and leave to chill.

3 Stretch out the bacon with the back of a knife and cut each slice into 2. Remove the chicken liver from the marinade, reserving the marinade for basting. Wrap the bacon around half of the chicken liver pieces. Thread the bacon and chicken liver rolls and the plain chicken liver pieces alternately on to 6 pre-soaked wooden skewers.

4 Barbecue (grill) the skewers over hot coals for 10-12 minutes, turning and basting with the reserved marinade frequently.

5 Meanwhile, cut the bread into 6 pieces and toast the cut sides on the barbecue (grill) until golden brown.

6 To serve, top the toasted bread with spinach leaves and place the kebabs (kabobs) on top. Spoon over the mustard mayonnaise and serve immediately.

COOK'S TIP

Take care not to overcook the chicken livers or they will become tough. They should be firm to the touch and just pink inside.

Citrus Duckling Skewers

The tartness of citrus fruit goes well with the rich meat of duckling.

Serves 12

INGREDIENTS

3 duckling breasts, skinned and
 boned
1 small red onion, cut into wedges
1 small aubergine (eggplant), cut into
 cubes

lime and lemon wedges, to garnish
 (optional)

MARINADE:
grated rind and juice of 1 lemon
grated rind and juice of 1 lime

grated rind and juice of 1 orange
1 clove garlic, crushed
1 tsp dried oregano
2 tbsp olive oil
dash of Tabasco sauce

1 Cut the duckling into bite-size pieces and place them in a non-metallic bowl together with the prepared red onion and aubergine (eggplant).

2 To make the marinade, place the lemon, lime and orange rinds and juices, garlic, oregano, oil and Tabasco sauce in a screw-top jar and shake until well combined.

3 Pour the marinade over the duckling and vegetables and toss to coat. Leave to marinate for 30 minutes.

4 Remove the duckling and vegetables from the marinade, reserving the marinade for basting, and thread them on to skewers.

5 Barbecue (grill) the skewers on an oiled rack over medium hot coals, turning and basting frequently with the reserved marinade, for 15-20 minutes until the meat is cooked through.

6 Serve the kebabs (kabobs) garnished with lemon and lime wedges for squeezing, if using.

COOK'S TIP

For more zing add 1 teaspoon of chilli sauce to the marinade. The meat can be marinated for several hours, but it is best to marinate the vegetables separately for only about 30 minutes.

Sesame Orange Duckling

Moist and flavourful, this dish is reminiscent of duck
à la orange but the flavour is even better.

Serves 4

INGREDIENTS

4 tbsp soy sauce
2 tbsp fine-cut marmalade
2 tbsp orange juice
2 cloves garlic, crushed

1 cm/^{1}/$_2$ inch piece root (fresh) ginger, grated
1 tbsp sherry vinegar
4 duckling portions
2 oranges, sliced

4 tbsp sesame seeds

TO SERVE:
green salad leaves
fresh herbs

1 Mix together the soy sauce, marmalade, orange juice, garlic, ginger and vinegar in a small bowl until well combined.

2 Trim away any excess fat from the duckling portions.

3 Place the duckling portions in a shallow, non-metallic dish and pour over the orange mixture. Cover and leave to marinate for at least 2 hours.

4 Divide most of the orange slices among 4 double-thickness pieces of kitchen foil, reserving some orange slices to serve. Place a duckling portion on top of the oranges and pour some of the marinade over each portion. Fold over the foil to enclose the duckling completely.

5 Barbecue (grill) over hot coals for about 40 minutes or until the meat is just cooked.

6 Remove the foil parcels from the heat and sprinkle the skin of the duckling with the sesame seeds. Place the duckling, skin-side down, directly on the oiled rack over the hot coals and barbecue (grill) for a further 5 minutes until the skin is crisp. Serve with the orange slices, salad leaves and fresh herbs.

COOK'S TIP

Cooking the duckling in foil parcels keeps the meat deliciously moist and means that all the flavour of the marinade is retained. If you prefer, you can omit the foil and cook them directly on the rack. Turn and baste frequently until cooked. Sprinkle with sesame seeds for the last few minutes of cooking.

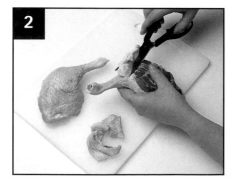

Barbecued (Grilled) Duckling

The sweet, spicy marinade used in this recipe gives the duckling a subtle flavour of the Orient.

Serves 4

INGREDIENTS

3 cloves garlic, crushed
150 ml/5 fl oz/^{2}/$_3$ cup light soy sauce
5 tbsp light muscovado sugar

2.5 cm/1 inch piece root (fresh)
  ginger, grated
1 tbsp chopped, fresh coriander
  (cilantro)

1 tsp five-spice powder
4 duckling breasts
sprig of fresh coriander (cilantro),
  to garnish

1 To make the marinade, mix together the garlic, soy sauce, sugar, grated ginger, chopped coriander (cilantro) and five-spice powder in a small bowl until well combined.

2 Place the duckling breasts in a shallow, non-metallic dish and pour over the marinade. Carefully turn over the duckling so that it is fully coated with the marinade on both sides.

3 Cover the bowl with cling film (plastic wrap) and leave to marinate for 1-6 hours, turning the duckling once or twice so that the marinade is fully absorbed.

4 Remove the duckling from the marinade, reserving the marinade for basting.

5 Barbecue (grill) the duckling breasts over hot coals for 20–30 minutes, turning and frequently basting with the reserved marinade.

6 Cut the duckling into slices and transfer to warm serving plates. Serve garnished with a sprig of fresh coriander (cilantro).

COOK'S TIP

Duckling is quite a fatty meat so there is no need to add oil to the marinade. However, you must remember to oil the barbecue (grill) rack to prevent the duckling from sticking. It is a good idea to oil the barbecue (grill) rack well away from the barbecue (grill) to avoid any danger of a flare-up.

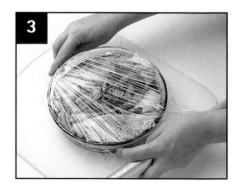

Glazed Duckling with Pineapple Salsa

A salsa is a cross between a sauce and a relish. Salsas are easy to prepare and will liven up all kinds of simple grilled (broiled) meats.

Serves 4

INGREDIENTS

2 tbsp Dijon mustard
1 tsp paprika
1/2 tsp ground ginger
1/2 tsp ground nutmeg
2 tbsp dark muscovado sugar

2 duckling halves
salad leaves, to serve

SALSA:
225 g/8 oz can pineapple in natural juice
2 tbsp dark muscovado sugar
1 small red onion, chopped finely
1 red chilli, deseeded and chopped

1 To make the salsa, drain the pineapple, reserving 2 tbsp of the juice. Finely chop the pineapple flesh.

2 Place the pineapple, reserved juice, sugar, onion and chilli in a bowl and mix well. Leave to stand for at least 1 hour for the flavours to fully develop.

3 Meanwhile, mix together the mustard, paprika, ginger, nutmeg and sugar. Spread the mixture evenly over the skin of the duckling halves.

4 Barbecue (grill) the duckling, skin-side up, over hot coals for about 30 minutes. Turn the duckling over and barbecue (grill) for 10–15 minutes or until the duckling is cooked through.

5 Serve with fresh salad leaves and the salsa.

COOK'S TIP

You could place the ducklings in a rectangular foil tray to protect the delicate flesh on the barbecue (grill).

VARIATION

Use canned apricots or peaches to make the salsa for a tasty alternative. The salsa is also delicious served with pork, lamb or chicken.

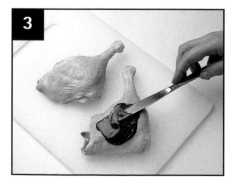

Meat

Most people think of meat when they think of barbecues (grills), and even the simplest chop tastes wonderful when cooked on the barbecue (grill). Add marinades or bastes, and you have the most appetizing meal you can imagine.

The following recipes include suggestions for all of your favourite cuts of meat, as well as new approaches to those barbecue (grill) favourites, burgers and sausages. Your only problem will be in deciding what not to cook. Don't be afraid of experimenting and mixing the bastes and marinades with different cuts and types of meat.

If you are having an impromptu barbecue (grill) choose recipes with a baste, although if time permits marinating meat not only adds flavour but helps to ensure that the meat is tender. Trim any excess fat from the meat so that it does not drip on to the coals, causing them to flare up – keep a water spray handy just in case.

Beef and lamb can be served pink in the centre, but you must make sure that pork is cooked thoroughly. Test it with a skewer to see if the juices run clear.

Beef Toppers

Beef burgers need never be dull when they are
accompanied with one of these tasty toppings.

Makes 6

INGREDIENTS

700 g/1 lb 9 oz minced lean beef
1 onion, chopped finely
2 tbsp Worcestershire sauce
salt and pepper
sesame baps, toasted, to serve

SAVOURY MUSHROOMS:
125 g/4 ¹/₂ oz button mushrooms,
　sliced
1 tbsp soy sauce
1 tbsp Worcestershire sauce

GUACAMOLE:
1 avocado
1 clove garlic

1 tbsp lemon juice
1 tbsp tomato relish

BARBECUE SAUCE:
3 tbsp brown fruity sauce
3 tbsp tomato ketchup (catsup)
1 tsp wholegrain mustard
1 tbsp clear honey

1 Choose one or all of the following toppings. To make the savoury mushrooms, combine all of the ingredients together and leave the mixture to marinate for at least 30 minutes.

2 To make the guacamole topping, peel, stone and mash the avocado. Mix the avocado with the garlic, lemon juice and tomato relish and leave to chill in the refrigerator until required.

3 To make the barbecue sauce, combine all of the ingredients together and leave to chill in the refrigerator until required.

4 To make the beefburgers, mix together the minced beef, onion, Worcestershire sauce and salt and pepper to taste until well combined. Divide into 6 portions and pat each into a neat round, about 1 cm/¹/₂ inch thick. Leave to chill for at least 30 minutes.

5 Barbecue (grill) over hot coals for 5-10 minutes on each side. Serve the burgers in the baps, with the topping spooned on top.

COOK'S TIP

A beefburger is only as good as the meat you use, so choose the best quality you can. For a more economical burger add 50 g/1 ³/₄ oz fresh breadcrumbs.

Beef Teriyaki

This Japanese-style teriyaki sauce complements beef
but it can also be used to accompany chicken or salmon.

Serves 4

INGREDIENTS

450 g/1 lb extra thin beef steaks
8 spring onions (scallions), trimmed
and cut into short lengths
1 yellow (bell) pepper, deseeded and
cut into chunks
green salad, to serve

SAUCE:
1 tsp cornflour (cornstarch)
2 tbsp dry sherry
2 tbsp white wine vinegar
3 tbsp soy sauce

1 tbsp dark muscovado sugar
1 clove garlic, crushed
$^1/_2$ tsp ground cinnamon
$^1/_2$ tsp ground ginger

1 Place the meat in a shallow, non-metallic dish.

2 To make the sauce, combine the cornflour (cornstarch) with the sherry, then stir in the remaining sauce ingredients. Pour the sauce over the meat and leave to marinate for at least 2 hours.

3 Remove the meat from the sauce and set aside. Pour the sauce into a small saucepan.

4 Cut the meat into thin strips and thread these, concertina-style, on to pre-soaked wooden skewers, alternating each strip of meat with the prepared pieces of (bell) pepper and spring onion (scallion).

5 Gently heat the sauce until it is just simmering, stirring occasionally.

6 Barbecue (grill) the kebabs (kabobs) over hot coals for 5–8 minutes, turning and basting the beef and vegetables occasionally with the reserved teriyaki sauce.

7 Arrange the skewers on serving plates and pour the remaining sauce over the kebabs (kabobs). Serve with a green salad.

COOK'S TIP

If you are short of time, omit the marinating, but the flavour will not permeate the meat as well.

Boozy Beef Steaks

A simple marinade gives plain steaks a fabulous flavour for very little effort.

Serves 4

INGREDIENTS

4 beef steaks
4 tbsp whisky or brandy
2 tbsp soy sauce

1 tbsp dark muscovado sugar
pepper
fresh sprig of parsley, to garnish

TO SERVE:
garlic bread
slices of tomato

1 Make a few cuts in the edge of fat on each steak. This will stop the meat curling as it cooks.

2 Place the meat in a shallow, non-metallic dish.

3 Combine the whisky or brandy, soy sauce, sugar and pepper to taste in a small bowl, stirring until the sugar dissolves. Pour the mixture over the steak. Cover and leave to marinate for at least 2 hours.

4 Barbecue (grill) the meat over hot coals, searing the meat over the hottest part of the barbecue (grill) for about 2 minutes on each side.

5 Move the meat to an area with slightly less intense heat and cook for a further 4–10 minutes on each side, depending on how well done you like your steaks. Test the meat is cooked by inserting the tip of a knife into the meat – the juices will run from red when the meat is still rare, to clear as it becomes well cooked.

6 Lightly barbecue (grill) the slices of tomato for 1–2 minutes.

7 Transfer the meat and the tomatoes to warm serving plates. Garnish with a sprig of fresh parsley and serve with garlic bread.

COOK'S TIP

Steaks are ideal for cooking on the barbecue (grill). Choose a good quality steak, such as fillet, rump, T-bone or entrecôte, with a light marbling of fat to prevent the meat from becoming too dry as it cooks. Quick-fry steaks can also be used, but these have to be pounded with a meat mallet to flatten and tenderize the meat.

Mexican Steaks with Avocado Salsa

Coated in Mexican spices and served with a refreshing avocado salsa, these steaks will pep up your barbecue (grill) fare.

Serves 4

INGREDIENTS

4 beef steaks
3 tbsp sunflower oil
1/2 red onion, grated
1 red chilli, deseeded and chopped finely
1 clove garlic, crushed
1 tbsp chopped, fresh coriander (cilantro)

1/2 tsp dried oregano
1 tsp ground cumin

AVOCADO SALSA:
1 ripe avocado
grated rind and juice of 1 lime
1 tbsp sunflower oil
1/2 red onion, chopped finely

1 red chilli, deseeded and chopped finely
1 tbsp chopped, fresh coriander (cilantro)
salt and pepper

1 Make a few cuts in the edge of fat around each steak to prevent the meat from curling as it cooks. Place the meat in a shallow, non-metallic dish.

2 Combine the oil, onion, chilli, garlic, coriander (cilantro), oregano and cumin in a small bowl. Pour the marinade over the steaks, turning the meat so that it is well coated. Leave to marinate for 1–2 hours.

3 To make the salsa, halve the avocado and remove the stone. Peel and cut the flesh into small dice. Combine the avocado with the lime rind and juice, oil, onion, chilli, coriander (cilantro) and salt and pepper to taste and mix well. Cover and leave to chill in the refrigerator until required.

4 Barbecue (grill) the steaks on an oiled rack over hot coals for 6–12 minutes on each side.

5 Serve the steaks accompanied with the avocado salsa.

VARIATION

The avocado salsa can also be served with chicken. Reduce the amount of chilli if you want a milder flavour. If fresh chillies are not available, look out for jars of minced chillies, which are a good substitute.

Barbecue Steaks with Red Onion Marmalade

Far from being sweet, this marmalade is a delicious savoury relish.

Serves 4

INGREDIENTS

4 rump steaks
2 tsp wholegrain mustard
2 tbsp sunflower oil
grated rind and juice of $1/2$ orange
salt and pepper

cooked new potatoes, to serve

RED ONION MARMALADE:
2 tbsp olive oil
450 g/1 lb red onions, cut into rings

200 ml/7 fl oz/$3/4$ cup red wine
rind of 1 orange, grated
1 tbsp caster (superfine) sugar

1 To make the marmalade, place the olive oil and onions in a saucepan and sauté gently for 5–10 minutes until the onions are just softened and are beginning to turn golden-brown – do not let them overcook.

2 Add the wine, orange rind and sugar to the pan and simmer for 10–15 minutes until the onions are tender and most of the liquid has evaporated. Leave to cool, then season with salt and pepper to taste.

3 Make a few cuts in the edge of fat around each steak to prevent the meat from curling as it cooks.

4 Using a knife, spread each steak with a little of the mustard and season with salt and pepper to taste.

5 Mix together the oil and the orange juice and rind in a small bowl, and use this mixture to baste the steaks occasionally during cooking.

6 Barbecue (grill) the steaks over hot coals, searing the meat over the hottest part of the barbecue (grill) for 2 minutes on each side, basting occasionally with the orange mixture. Move the meat to an area with slightly less intense heat and cook, basting occasionally, for 4–10 minutes on each side, depending on how well done you like your steaks.

7 Transfer the steaks to plates and serve with the red onion marmalade and new potatoes.

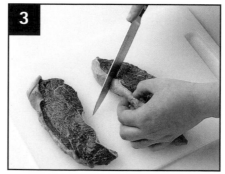

Surf & Turf Kebabs (Kabobs)

This dish originated in Australia. The name refers to the prawns (shrimp) from the sea – the 'surf' - and the meat from the land – the 'turf'.

Makes 6

INGREDIENTS

450 g/1 lb rump or sirloin steak
18 raw prawns (shrimp)

MARINADE:
5 tbsp oyster sauce
1 tbsp soy sauce

3 tbsp lemon juice
4 tbsp sunflower oil

1 Cut the steaks into 24 evenly-sized pieces and place the meat in a non-metallic dish.

2 Peel the prawns (shrimp), leaving the tail attached, as these look attractive.

3 To make the marinade, combine the oyster sauce, soy sauce, lemon juice and sunflower oil in a small bowl. Pour the mixture over the meat and leave to marinate for 15 minutes.

4 Add the prawns (shrimp) to the marinade, toss to coat, and let marinate for 5 minutes.

5 Remove the meat and prawns from the marinade, reserving the marinade for basting. Thread the meat on to metal or pre-soaked wooden skewers, alternating the steak with the prawns (shrimp). (Pre-soaking wooden skewers helps to prevent them from burning as the meat cooks.)

6 Barbecue (grill) the kebabs (kabobs) over hot coals for 5–10 minutes, basting with the reserved marinade and turning frequently.

7 Transfer the kebabs (kabobs) to warm serving plates.

VARIATION

Other shellfish, such as lobster and crab, can be added to the skewers. These kebabs (kabobs) are also delicious marinated in, and basted with, a herb, garlic and oil marinade.

Beef Tomato & Olive Kebabs (Kabobs)

These kebabs (kabobs) have a Mediterranean flavour. The sweetness of the tomatoes and the sharpness of the olives makes them rather more-ish.

Serves 8

INGREDIENTS

450 g/1 lb rump or sirloin steak
16 cherry tomatoes
16 large green olives, pitted
focaccia bread, to serve

BASTE:
4 tbsp olive oil

1 tbsp sherry vinegar
1 clove garlic, crushed
salt and freshly ground black pepper

FRESH TOMATO RELISH:
1 tbsp olive oil
1/2 red onion, chopped finely

1 clove garlic, chopped
6 plum tomatoes, deseeded, skinned
 and chopped
2 pitted green olives, sliced
1 tbsp chopped, fresh parsley
1 tbsp lemon juice

1 Trim any fat from the beef and cut the meat into about 24 evenly-sized pieces.

2 Thread the meat on to 8 skewers, alternating the meat with cherry tomatoes and olives.

3 To make the baste, combine the oil, vinegar, garlic and salt and pepper to taste in a bowl.

4 To make the relish, heat the oil in a small pan and fry the onion and garlic for 3–4 minutes until softened. Add the tomatoes and olives and cook for 2–3 minutes until the tomatoes are softened slightly. Stir in the parsley and lemon juice and season with salt and pepper to taste. Set aside and keep warm or leave to chill.

5 Barbecue (grill) the skewers on an oiled rack over hot coals for 5–10 minutes, basting and turning frequently. Serve with the tomato relish and slices of focaccia.

COOK'S TIP

The kebabs (kabobs), baste and relish can be prepared several hours in advance, avoiding the need for any last minute rush. For a simple meal, serve with crusty fresh bread and a mixed salad.

Beef with Wild Mushrooms

Choose thick steaks for this dish – it will be easier to cut the pockets in the side of each one.

Serves 4

INGREDIENTS

4 steaks, fillet or sirloin	150 g/5 ¹/₂ oz mixed wild	TO SERVE:
50 g/1 ³/₄ oz butter	mushrooms	salad leaves
1–2 cloves garlic, crushed	2 tbsp chopped, fresh parsley	cherry tomatoes, halved

1 Place the steaks on to a chopping board and using a sharp knife, cut a pocket into the side of each steak.

2 To make the stuffing, heat the butter in a frying pan, add the garlic and fry gently for about 1 minute.

3 Add the mushrooms to the pan and sauté gently for 4–6 minutes until tender. Stir in the parsley.

4 Divide the mushroom mixture into 4 and insert a portion into the pocket of each steak. Seal the pocket closed with a cocktail stick (toothpick). If preparing ahead, allow the mixture to cool before stuffing the steaks.

5 Barbecue (grill) the steaks over hot coals, searing the meat over the hottest part of the barbecue (grill) for about 2 minutes on each side. Move the steaks to an area with slightly less intense heat and barbecue (grill) for a further 4–10 minutes on each side, depending on how well done you like your steaks.

6 Transfer the steaks to serving plates and remove the cocktail sticks (toothpicks). Serve with salad leaves and cherry tomatoes.

COOK'S TIP

Wild mushrooms, such as shiitake, oyster and chanterelle, are now readily available in supermarkets. Look out for boxes of mixed wild mushrooms, which are usually cheaper than buying the different types individually.

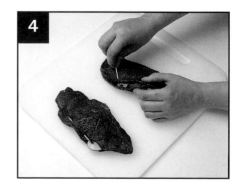

Meatball Brochettes

Children will love these tasty meatballs on a skewer, which are economical and easy to make.

Makes 8

INGREDIENTS

25 g/1 oz cracked wheat
350 g/12 oz lean minced beef
1 onion, chopped very finely
    (optional)

1 tbsp tomato ketchup (catsup)
1 tbsp brown fruity sauce
1 tbsp chopped, fresh parsley
beaten egg, to bind

8 cherry tomatoes
8 button mushrooms
oil, to baste
8 bread finger rolls, to serve

1 Place the cracked wheat in a bowl and cover with boiling water. Leave to soak for 20 minutes or until softened. Drain thoroughly and leave to cool.

2 Place the wheat, minced beef, onion (if using), ketchup (catsup), brown sauce and parsley together in a mixing bowl and mix well. Add a little beaten egg if necessary to bind the mixture together.

3 Using your hands, shape the meat mixture into 18 even-sized balls. Leave to chill in the refrigerator for 30 minutes.

4 Thread the meatballs on to 8 pre-soaked wooden skewers, alternating them with the cherry tomatoes and button mushrooms.

5 Brush the kebabs (kabobs) with a little oil and barbecue (grill) over hot coals for about 10 minutes, turning occasionally and brushing with a little more oil if necessary.

6 Transfer the kebabs (kabobs) to warm serving plates. Cut open the bread finger rolls and push the meat and vegetables off the skewer into the open rolls to serve, if you wish.

COOK'S TIP

The cracked wheat 'stretches' the beef, making this a cheap and cheerful meal. It also produces a less dense meatball with a nutty texture that children often like.

Char-grilled Venison Steaks

*Venison has a good strong flavour, which makes it an ideal meat
to barbecue (grill). Marinate overnight to tenderize the meat.*

Serves 4

INGREDIENTS

4 venison steaks
150 ml/5 fl oz/²/₃ cup red wine
2 tbsp sunflower oil
1 tbsp red wine vinegar
1 onion, chopped

few sprigs fresh parsley
2 sprigs fresh thyme
1 bay leaf
1 tsp caster (superfine) sugar
¹/₂ tsp mild mustard

salt and pepper

TO SERVE:
jacket potatoes
salad leaves and cherry tomatoes

1 Place the venison steaks in a shallow, non-metallic dish.

2 Combine the wine, oil, wine vinegar, onion, fresh parsley, thyme, bay leaf, sugar, mustard and salt and pepper to taste in a screw-top jar and shake vigorously until well combined. Alternatively, using a fork, whisk the ingredients together in a bowl.

3 Pour the marinade mixture over the venison, cover and leave to marinate in the refrigerator overnight. Turn the steaks over in the mixture occasionally so that the meat is well coated.

4 Barbecue (grill) the venison over hot coals, searing the meat over the hottest part of the barbecue (grill) for about 2 minutes on each side.

5 Move the meat to an area with slightly less intense heat and barbecue (grill) for a further 4–10 minutes on each side, depending on how well done you like your steaks. Test if the meat is cooked by inserting the tip of a knife into the meat – the juices will run from red when the meat is still rare to clear as the meat becomes well cooked.

6 Serve with jacket potateoes, salad leaves and tomatoes.

COOK'S TIP

Farmed venison is available all year round. Look out for it in the meat section of the supermarket or order it from an independent butcher. This dish is also delicious when served with red onion marmalade (see page 104).

Lamb Burgers with Mint & Pine Nuts

*These tasty burgers have a Greek flavour. Serve them
in the traditional soft bap or in pitta breads.*

Serves 4

INGREDIENTS

450 g/1 lb lean minced lamb
1 small onion, chopped finely
50 g/1³/₄ oz pine nuts

2 tbsp chopped, fresh mint
salt and pepper

TO SERVE:
4 pitta breads or soft baps
75 g/2 ³/₄oz Feta cheese
salad leaves

1 Place the minced lamb, chopped onion, pine nuts, fresh mint and salt and pepper to taste in a large bowl and mix together until thoroughly combined.

2 Using your hands, divide the mixture into 4 and shape the portions into round burgers, pressing the mixture together well. Leave to chill in the refrigerator for 30 minutes.

3 Barbecue (grill) the burgers over hot coals for 4–5 minutes on each side, turning once, until the juices run clear.

4 Warm the pitta breads at the side of the barbecue or toast the baps.

5 Crumble the Feta cheese into small pieces and set aside until required.

6 Line the pitta bread or baps with the salad leaves. Sandwich the burgers between the pitta bread or baps, and top with the crumbled Feta cheese.

COOK'S TIP

If you do not have any fresh mint, use 1–2 teaspoons of mint sauce, which has a much fresher taste than dried mint. Leave the burgers to chill in the refrigerator before cooking them so that they become firmer and are far less likely to fall apart.

Butterfly Chops with Redcurrant Glaze

A butterfly chop is a double chop cut across the saddle. They make an attractive cut, but you can use single chops if you prefer.

Serves 4

INGREDIENTS

4 tbsp redcurrant jelly
2 tbsp raspberry vinegar
1/2 tsp dried rosemary
1 clove garlic, crushed

1 tbsp sunflower oil
4 butterfly lamb chops or 8 loin lamb chops

4 baby aubergines (eggplant)
oil, to basting

1 To make the glaze, combine the redcurrant jelly, vinegar, rosemary, garlic and oil in a small pan and heat, stirring occasionally, until the jelly melts and the ingredients are well blended.

2 Barbecue (grill) the chops over hot coals for 5 minutes on each side.

3 Cut each aubergine (eggplant) in half and brush the cut sides liberally with oil.

4 Barbecue (grill) the aubergine (eggplant) alongside the lamb for 3–4 minutes on each side or until cooked through. Set aside and keep warm.

5 Brush the glaze over the chops and barbecue (grill) the meat for a further 5 minutes on each side, basting frequently, until the meat is cooked. Keep the redcurrant glaze warm at the side of the barbecue (grill).

6 Transfer the lamb and aubergines (eggplants) to warm serving plates and pour over the remaining redcurrant glaze. Serve immediately.

VARIATION

You can use other lamb cuts for this dish – leg steaks or chump chops are ideal. The redcurrant glaze also goes well with chicken; par-boil or microwave chicken drumsticks, then brush them with the redcurrant glaze and finish off on the barbecue (grill).

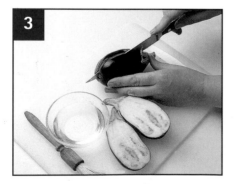

Lamb with a Spice Crust

*Lamb neck fillet is a tender cut that is not too thick and is,
therefore, ideal for cooking on the barbecue.*

Serves 4

INGREDIENTS

1 tbsp olive oil
2 tbsp light muscovado sugar
2 tbsp wholegrain mustard

1 tbsp horseradish sauce
1 tbsp plain (all-purpose) flour
350 g/12 oz neck fillet of lamb
salt and pepper

TO SERVE:
coleslaw
slices of tomato

1 Combine the oil, sugar, mustard, horseradish sauce, flour and salt and pepper to taste in a shallow, non-metallic dish until they are well mixed.

2 Roll the lamb in the spice mixture until well coated.

3 Lightly oil one or two pieces of foil or a large, double thickness of foil. Place the lamb on the foil and wrap it up so that the meat is completely enclosed.

4 Place the foil parcel over hot coals for 30 minutes, turning the parcel over occasionally.

5 Open the kitchen foil, spoon the cooking juices over the lamb and continue to barbecue (grill) for a further 10-15 minutes or until cooked through.

6 Transfer the lamb to a warm serving plate and remove the foil. Cut the lamb into thick slices and serve with coleslaw and a few slices of tomato.

COOK'S TIP

Lamb is naturally fatter than beef, which makes it a good choice for cooking on the barbecue (grill).

COOK'S TIP

If preferred, the lamb can be completely removed from the kitchen foil for the second part of the cooking. Barbecue (grill) the lamb directly over the coals for a smokier barbecue (grill) flavour, basting with extra oil if necessary.

Kibbeh

This Lebanese dish is similar to the Turkish kofte and the Indian kofta,
but the spices used to flavour the meat are quite different.

Makes 8

INGREDIENTS

75 g/2¾ oz couscous
1 small onion
350 g/12 oz lean minced lamb
½ tsp ground cinnamon

¼ tsp cayenne
4 tsp ground allspice
green salad and onion rings, to serve

BASTE:
2 tbsp tomato ketchup (catsup)
2 tbsp sunflower oil

1 Place the couscous in a large bowl, cover with cold water and leave to stand for 30 minutes or until the couscous has swelled and softened. Alternatively, soak the couscous according to the instructions on the packet.

2 Drain the couscous through a sieve and squeeze out as much moisture as you can.

3 If you have a food processor, add the onion and chop finely. Add the lamb and process briefly to chop the mince further. If you do not have a processor, grate the onion before mixing with the lamb.

4 Combine the couscous, lamb and spices and mix well. Divide the mixture into 8 equal sized portions. Press and shape the mixture around 8 skewers, pressing the mixture together firmly so that it holds it shape. Leave to chill for 30 minutes.

5 To make the baste, combine the oil and ketchup (catsup).

6 Barbecue (grill) the kibbeh over hot coals for 10–15 minutes, turning and basting frequently. Serve with barbecued (grilled) onion rings and green salad leaves.

VARIATION

The spicy baste used in this recipe also works well with barbecued (grilled) vegetables.

COOK'S TIP

Putting the minced lamb through the food processor chops it further and helps the mixture hold together better. Adding couscous to a mince mixture 'stretches' the meat, making the dish very economical to make. You can add it to other types of mince and use it to make kebabs or burgers.

Barbecued (Grilled) Lamb Ribs

*These sweet and spicy lamb ribs are best eaten with your fingers.
Make sure there are plenty napkins available.*

Serves 4

INGREDIENTS

breast of lamb, about 700 g/1 lb 9 oz
3 tbsp sweet chutney (relish)
4 tbsp tomato ketchup (catsup)
2 tbsp cider vinegar

2 tsp Worcestershire sauce
2 tsp mild mustard
1 tbsp light muscovado sugar

TO SERVE:
salad leaves
cherry tomatoes

1 Using a sharp knife, cut between the ribs of the breast of lamb to divide it into slightly smaller pieces.

2 Bring a large saucepan of water to the boil, add the lamb and par-cook for about 5 minutes. Remove the meat from the water and pat dry thoroughly with paper towels.

3 Combine the sweet chutney (relish), tomato ketchup (catsup), cider vinegar, Worcestershire sauce, mustard and sugar in a shallow, non-metallic dish to make a sauce.

4 Using a sharp knife, cut the lamb into individual ribs. Add the ribs to the sauce and toss until well coated.

5 Remove the ribs from the sauce, reserving the remaining sauce for basting.

6 Barbecue (grill) the ribs over hot coals for 10-15 minutes, turning and basting frequently with the reserved sauce.

7 Transfer the ribs to warm serving plates. Serve immediately with salad leaves and cherry tomatoes.

VARIATION

Use pork belly strips if you prefer and, as with the lamb, par-cook the pork to remove some of the excess fat from the meat.

COOK'S TIP

If you are short of time, look out for ready-prepared lamb's ribs – they are widely available in most large supermarkets.

Butterfly Lamb with Balsamic Vinegar & Mint

*The appearance of the leg of lamb as it is opened out
to cook on the barbecue (grill) gives this dish its name.*

Serves 4

INGREDIENTS

boned leg of lamb, about 1.8 kg/4 lb
8 tbsp balsamic vinegar
grated rind and juice of 1 lemon
150 ml/5 fl oz/²/₃ cup sunflower oil

4 tbsp chopped, fresh mint
2 cloves garlic, crushed
2 tbsp light muscovado sugar
salt and pepper

TO SERVE:
grilled vegetables
green salad leaves

1 Open out the boned leg of lamb so that its shape resembles a butterfly. Thread 2–3 skewers through the meat to make it easier to turn on the barbecue (grill).

2 Combine the balsamic vinegar, lemon rind and juice, oil, mint, garlic, sugar and salt and pepper to taste in a non-metallic dish that is large enough to hold the lamb.

3 Place the lamb in the dish and turn it over a few times so that the meat is coated on both sides with the marinade. Leave to marinate for at least 6 hours or preferably overnight, turning occasionally.

4 Remove the lamb from the marinade and reserve the liquid for basting.

5 Place the rack about 15 cm/ 6 inches above the coals and barbecue (grill) the lamb for about 30 minutes on each side, turning once and basting frequently with the marinade.

6 Transfer the lamb to a chopping board and remove the skewers. Cut the lamb into slices across the grain and serve with grilled vegetables and green salad leaves.

COOK'S TIP

*If you prefer, cook the lamb for half
the cooking time in a preheated
oven at 180°C/350°F/
Gas Mark 4, then finish off on
the barbecue (grill).*

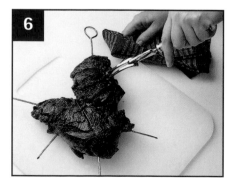

Red Wine Lamb Skewers

*Use the best quality red wine you can afford. Instead of using fresh herbs,
add a bouquet garni to the marinade, if you prefer.*

Makes 4

INGREDIENTS

450 g/1 lb lean lamb
12 button onions or shallots
12 button mushrooms
salad leaves and cherry tomatoes,
   to serve

MARINADE:
150 ml/5 fl oz/²/₃ cup red wine
4 tbsp olive oil
2 tbsp brandy (optional)

1 onion, sliced
1 bay leaf
sprig of fresh thyme
2 sprigs fresh parsley

1 Carefully trim away any excess fat from the lamb. Cut the lamb into large pieces.

2 To make the marinade, combine the wine, oil, brandy (if using), onion, bay leaf, thyme and parsley in a non-metallic dish.

3 Add the meat to the dish and toss to coat the meat thoroughly in the marinade. Cover the dish and leave to marinate in the refrigerator for at least 2 hours or preferably overnight.

4 Bring a pan of water to a rolling boil, drop in the unpeeled button onions and blanch them for 3 minutes. Drain and refresh the onions under cold water, and then drain again. Trim the onions and remove their skins, which will now slip off easily.

5 Remove the meat from the marinade, reserving the liquid for basting. Thread the meat on to skewers, alternating with the button onions and mushrooms.

6 Barbecue (grill) the kebabs (kabobs) over hot coals for 8–10 minutes, turning and basting the meat and vegetables with the reserved marinade a few times.

7 Transfer the lamb kebabs (kabobs) to a warm serving plate and serve with fresh salad leaves and cherry tomatoes.

VARIATION

This recipe also works well with beef. Bacon rolls can also be added to the skewers, if you like.

Moroccan Lamb Kebabs (Kabobs)

Marinated in Moroccan spices, these kebabs (kabobs) have a mild spicy flavour.
Add the chilli if you like a bit of zip to your meat.

Makes 4

INGREDIENTS

450 g/1 lb lean lamb
1 lemon
1 red onion
4 small courgettes (zucchini)
couscous, to serve (see Cook's Tip)

MARINADE:
grated rind and juice of 1 lemon
2 tbsp olive oil
1 clove garlic, crushed
1 red chilli, sliced (optional)

1 tsp ground cinnamon
1 tsp ground ginger
1/2 tsp ground cumin
1/2 tsp ground coriander

1 Cut the lamb into large, evenly-sized chunks.

2 To make the marinade, combine the lemon rind and juice, oil, garlic, chilli (if using), ground cinnamon, ginger, cumin and coriander in a large non-metallic dish.

3 Add the meat to the marinade, tossing to coat the meat completely. Cover and leave to marinate in the refrigerator for at least 2 hours or preferably overnight.

4 Cut the lemon into 8 pieces. Cut the onion into wedges, then separate each wedge into 2 pieces.

5 Using a canelle knife (or potato peeler), cut thin strips of peel from the courgettes (zucchini), then cut the courgettes (zucchini) into chunks.

6 Remove the meat from the marinade, reserving the liquid for basting. Thread the meat on to skewers alternating with the onion, lemon and courgette (zucchini).

7 Barbecue (grill) over hot coals for 8–10 minutes, turning and basting with the reserved marinade. Serve on a bed of couscous (see Cook's Tip, below).

COOK'S TIP

Serve these kebabs with couscous or tabouleh. Allowing 60 g/2 oz couscous per person, soak the couscous in cold water for about 20 minutes until the grains have softened. Drain and steam for 10 minutes or until piping hot.

Shish Kebabs (Kabobs)

The name of this dish derives from the Turkish words sis *(skewer) and* kebap *(roast meat).*
A favourite take-away, these kebabs (kabobs) are easy to make at home.

Makes 4

INGREDIENTS

50 g/1 lb lean lamb
1 red onion, cut into wedges
1 green (bell) pepper, deseeded

MARINADE:
1 onion

4 tbsp olive oil
grated rind and juice of $^{1}/_{2}$ lemon
1 clove garlic, crushed
$^{1}/_{2}$ tsp dried oregano
$^{1}/_{2}$tsp dried thyme

TO SERVE:
4 pitta breads
2 tomatoes, sliced
few crisp lettuce leaves, shredded
chilli sauce (optional)

1 Cut the lamb into large, evenly-sized chunks.

2 To make the marinade, grate the onion or chop it very finely in a food processor. Remove the juice by squeezing the onion between two plates set over a small bowl to collect the juice.

3 Combine the onion juice with the remaining marinade ingredients in a non-metallic dish and add the meat. Toss the meat in the marinade, cover and leave to marinate in the refrigerator for at least 2 hours or overnight .

4 Divide the onion wedges into 2. Cut the (bell) peppers into chunks.

5 Remove the meat from the marinade, reserving the liquid for basting. Thread the meat on to skewers, alternating with the onion and (bell) peppers. Barbecue (grill) over hot coals for 8–10 minutes, turning and basting with the reserved marinade.

6 Split open the pitta breads and fill with a little lettuce. Serve the kebabs (kabobs) in the bread, pushing the meat and vegetables off the skewers as you do so. Top with tomatoes and chilli sauce.

VARIATION

These kebabs (kabobs) are delicious served with saffron-flavoured rice and a mixed salad. For easy saffron rice, simply use saffron stock cubes when cooking the rice.

Lamb Cutlets with Rosemary

A classic combination of flavours, this dish would make a perfect Sunday lunch.
Serve with tomato and onion salad and jacket potatoes.

Serves 4

INGREDIENTS

8 lamb cutlets
5 tbsp olive oil
2 tbsp lemon juice
1 clove garlic, crushed
$1/2$ tsp lemon pepper
salt
8 sprigs rosemary

jacket potatoes, to serve

SALAD:
4 tomatoes, sliced
4 spring onions (scallion), sliced
 diagonally

DRESSING:
2 tbsp olive oil
1 tbsp lemon juice
1 clove garlic, chopped
$1/4$ tsp fresh rosemary, chopped finely

1 Trim the lamb chops by cutting away the flesh with a sharp knife to expose the tips of the bones.

2 Place the oil, lemon juice garlic, lemon pepper and salt in a shallow, non-metallic dish and whisk with a fork to combine.

3 Lay the sprigs of rosemary in the dish and place the lamb on top. Leave to marinate for at least 1 hour, turning the lamb cutlets once.

4 Remove the chops from the marinade and wrap a little kitchen foil around the bones to stop them from burning.

5 Place the sprigs of rosemary on the rack and place the lamb on top. Barbecue (grill) for 10–15 minutes, turning once.

6 Meanwhile make the salad and dressing. Arrange the tomatoes on a serving dish and scatter the spring onions (scallions) on top. Place all the ingredients for the dressing in a screw-top jar, shake well and pour over the salad. Serve with the barbecued (grilled) lamb cutlets and jacket potatoes.

COOK'S TIP

Choose medium to small baking potatoes if you want to cook jacket potatoes on the barbecue (grill). Scrub them well, prick with a fork and wrap in buttered kitchen foil. Bury them in the hot coals and barbecue (grill) for 50–60 minutes.

Lamb with Mango & Chilli

These lamb chops really pack a punch when they are served with a hot spicy mango relish.

Serves 4

INGREDIENTS

4 chump lamb chops
4 tbsp mango chutney (relish)
2 tsp chilli sauce
grilled vegetables, to serve

SPICY MANGO RELISH:
1 ripe mango
2 tbsp cider vinegar

2 tbsp light muscovado sugar
$\frac{1}{2}$ tsp ground cinnamon
$\frac{1}{2}$ tsp ground ginger

1 To make the spicy mango relish, cut the mango lengthwise down both sides of the large, flat stone and discard the stone. Peel the mango and cut the flesh into evenly-sized chunks.

2 Place the cider vinegar, sugar, cinnamon and spices in a small pan and heat gently, stirring continuously, until the sugar dissolves.

3 Stir the mango into the mixture in the pan and cook gently at the side of the barbecue (grill) or on the stove for about 5 minutes or until the mango is soft.

4 Barbecue (grill) the chops on an oiled rack for about 4 minutes on each side.

5 Combine the mango chutney (relish) and chilli sauce in a small bowl and brush the glaze over the chops.

6 Continue to barbecue (grill) for a further 2–5 minutes on each side until the lamb is cooked, turning and basting frequently with the mango chutney (relish) and chilli glaze.

7 Serve with grilled vegetables and the spicy mango relish.

VARIATION

The spicy mango relish can also be served cold. Simmer the combined ingredients for 5 minutes, then remove from the heat and allow to cool. Leave to chill in the refrigerator until required. You can also use the mango chutney (relish) and chilli glaze on other cuts of lamb or on pork chops.

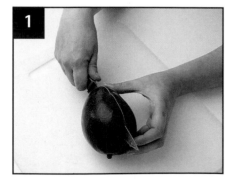

Indian Kofta

Lean minced lamb is mixed with curry paste to produce a flavourful Indian-style kebab (kabob), which is served with a refreshing tomato sambal.

Makes 8

INGREDIENTS

1 small onion
450 g/1 lb minced lamb
2 tbsp curry paste
2 tbsp natural yogurt
oil, to baste
sprigs of fresh coriander (cilantro),
   to garnish

TOMATO SAMBAL:
3 tomatoes, deseeded and diced
pinch of ground coriander
pinch of ground cumin
2 tsp chopped, fresh coriander
   (cilantro)
salt and pepper

TO SERVE:
poppadoms
chutney (relish)

1 Put the onion in a food processor and chop finely. Add the lamb and process briefly to chop the mince further. Chopping the mince again will help the meat mixture to hold together during cooking. If you do not have a food processor, grate the onion finely before mixing it with the lamb.

2 Add the curry paste and yogurt and mix well. Divide the mixture into 8 equal portions.

3 Press and shape the mixture into 8 sausage shapes and push each one on to a skewer, pressing the mixture together firmly so that it holds its shape. Leave to chill in the refrigerator for at least 30 minutes or until required.

4 To make the tomato sambal, mix together the tomatoes, spices, chopped coriander (cilantro) and salt and pepper to taste in a bowl. Leave to stand for at least 30 minutes for the flavours to combine.

5 Barbecue (grill) the kebabs (kabobs) on an oiled rack over hot coals for 10–15 minutes, turning frequently. Baste with a little oil if required.

6 Transfer to serving plates and garnish with fresh coriander (cilantro). Serve accompanied with poppadoms, chutney (relish) and the tomato sambal.

Sweet Lamb Fillet

Lamb fillet, enhanced by a sweet and spicy glaze, is cooked in a kitchen foil parcel for deliciously moist results.

Serves 4

INGREDIENTS

2 fillets of neck of lamb, each 225 g/
  8 oz
1 tbsp olive oil
1/2 onion, chopped finely
1 clove garlic, crushed

2.5 cm/1 inch piece root (fresh)
  ginger, grated
5 tbsp apple juice
3 tbsp smooth apple sauce
1 tbsp light muscovado sugar

1 tbsp tomato ketchup (catsup)
1/2 tsp mild mustard
salt and pepper
green salad leaves, croûtons and
  fresh crusty bread, to serve

1 Place the lamb fillet on a large piece of double thickness kitchen foil. Season with salt and pepper to taste.

2 Heat the oil in a small pan and fry the onion and garlic for 2–3 minutes until softened but not browned. Stir in the grated ginger and cook for 1 minute, stirring occasionally.

3 Stir in the apple juice, apple sauce, sugar, ketchup (catsup) and mustard and bring to the boil. Boil rapidly for about 10 minutes until reduced by half. Stir the mixture occasionally so that it does not burn and stick to the base of the pan.

4 Brush half of the sauce over the lamb, then wrap up the lamb in the kitchen foil to completely enclose it. Barbecue (grill) over hot coals for about 25 minutes, turning the parcel over occasionally.

5 Open out the kitchen foil and brush the lamb with some of the sauce. Continue to barbecue (grill) for a further 15–20 minutes or until cooked through.

6 Place the lamb on a chopping board, remove the foil and cut into thick slices. Transfer to serving plates and spoon over the remaining sauce. Serve with green salad leaves, croûtons and fresh crusty bread.

COOK'S TIP

If you prefer, you can cook the lamb for the first part of the cooking time in a preheated oven at 180°C/350°F/Gas Mark 4. Place the kitchen foil parcel in a baking dish to avoid any leakages.

Lamb Noisettes with Tomato Salsa

*Here, the lamb is served with a fragrant tomato side dish. If you like your meals
a little spicy, add chilli sauce to both the salsa and the marinade.*

Serves 4

INGREDIENTS

8 lamb noisettes
4 basil leaves
2 tbsp olive oil
grated rind and juice of ¹/₂ lime
salt and pepper

sprig of fresh basil, to garnish
green salad leaves, to serve

SALSA:
6 tomatoes

4 basil leaves
8 stuffed green olives
1 tbsp lime juice
pinch of caster (superfine) sugar

1 Place the lamb noisettes in a shallow, non-metallic dish. Tear the basil leaves into pieces and scatter them over the lamb.

2 Drizzle the oil and lime juice over the lamb and add the lime rind. Season with salt and pepper to taste. Cover and leave to marinate in the refrigerator for at least 1 hour or preferably overnight.

3 To make the salsa, skin the tomatoes by cutting a small cross at the stem. Drop the tomatoes into boiling water for

about 30 seconds, remove with a perforated spoon and then peel off the skins.

4 Cut the tomatoes in half, then scoop out the seeds and discard them. Cut the tomato flesh into large dice. Tear the basil leaves into pieces. Chop the olives. Mix together the tomatoes, basil, olives, lime juice and sugar in a bowl and leave for at least 1 hour or until required.

5 Remove the lamb from the marinade, reserving the marinade for basting. Barbecue

(grill) over hot coals for 10–15 minutes, turning once and basting with the reserved marinade.

6 Garnish with a sprig of basil and serve with the tomato salsa and green salad leaves.

COOK'S TIP

Green olives are picked and processed before they have ripened. Some are pickled and stuffed, usually with a little red pimento or a slither of almond. Use either in this recipe and chop the stuffing.

Caribbean Pork

*Serve these tasty marinated pork chops with a coconut-flavoured savoury rice
and accompanied with Spicy Sweet Potato Slices (page 178).*

Serves 4

INGREDIENTS

4 pork loin chops
4 tbsp dark muscovado sugar
4 tbsp orange or pineapple juice
2 tbsp Jamaican rum
1 tbsp desiccated (shredded) coconut
$^1/_2$ tsp ground cinnamon

mixed salad leaves, to serve

COCONUT RICE:
225 g/8 oz/1 cup Basmati rice
450 ml/16 fl oz/2 cups water
150 ml/5 fl oz/$^2/_3$ cup coconut milk

4 tbsp raisins
4 tbsp roasted peanuts or cashew
    nuts
salt and pepper
2 tbsp desiccated (shredded) coconut,
    toasted

1 Trim any excess fat from the pork and place the chops in a shallow, non-metallic dish.

2 Combine the sugar, fruit juice, rum, coconut and cinnamon in a bowl, stirring until the sugar dissolves. Pour the mixture over the pork and leave to marinate in the refrigerator for at least 2 hours or preferably overnight.

3 Remove the pork from the marinade, reserving the liquid for basting. Barbecue (grill) over hot coals for 15–20 minutes, basting with the marinade.

4 Meanwhile, make the coconut rice. Rinse the rice under cold water, place it in a pan with the water and coconut milk and bring gently to the boil. Stir, cover and reduce the heat. Simmer gently for 12 minutes or until the rice is tender and the liquid has been absorbed. Fluff up with a fork.

5 Stir the raisins and nuts into the rice, season with salt and pepper to taste and sprinkle with the coconut. Transfer the pork and rice to warm serving plates and serve with the mixed salad leaves.

VARIATION

These pork chops are delicious served with barbecued (grilled) pineapple slices. Sprinkle the pineapple with dark muscovado sugar and cinnamon. Barbecue (grill) over hot coals for 5 minutes, turning once, until piping hot.

Ham Steaks with Spicy Apple Rings

This dish is quick to prepare because there is no marinating involved. Ham has a good, strong flavour and cooks well on the barbecue (grill).

Serves 4

INGREDIENTS

4 ham steaks, each about 175 g/6 oz
1–2 tsp wholegrain mustard
1 tbsp honey
2 tbsp lemon juice
1 tbsp sunflower oil

APPLE RINGS:
2 green dessert (eating) apples
2 tsp demerara sugar
$^1/_4$ tsp ground nutmeg
$^1/_4$ tsp ground cinnamon

$^1/_4$ tsp ground allspice
1–2 tbsp melted butter

1 Using a pair of scissors, make a few cuts around the edges of the ham steaks to prevent them from curling up as they cook. Spread a little wholegrain mustard over the steaks.

2 Mix together the honey, lemon juice and oil in a bowl.

3 To prepare the apple rings, core the apples and cut them into thick slices. Mix the sugar with the spices and press the apple slices in the mixture until well coated on both sides.

4 Barbecue (grill) the steaks over hot coals for 3–4 minutes on each side, basting with the honey and lemon mixture to prevent the meat from drying out during cooking.

5 Brush the apple slices with a little melted butter and barbecue (grill) alongside the pork for 3–4 minutes, turning once and brushing with melted butter as they cook.

6 Serve the ham steaks with the apple slices as a garnish.

COOK'S TIP

Ham can be a little salty. If you have time, soak the steaks in cold water for 30–60 minutes before cooking – this process will remove the excess salt.

VARIATION

Pineapple rings can also be cooked in the same way as the apple rings for a delicious alternative garnish to this dish.

Pork & Apple Skewers with Mustard

*Flavoured with mustard and served with a mustard sauce, these kebabs (kabobs)
make an ideal lunch or they can be served as part of a large barbecue (grill) spread.*

Makes 4

INGREDIENTS

450 g/1 lb pork fillet
2 (dessert) eating apples
a little lemon juice
1 lemon

2 tsp wholegrain mustard
2 tsp Dijon mustard
2 tbsp apple or orange juice
2 tbsp sunflower oil
crusty brown bread, to serve

MUSTARD SAUCE:
1 tbsp wholegrain mustard
1 tsp Dijon mustard
6 tbsp single (light) cream

1 To make the mustard sauce, combine the wholegrain and Dijon mustards in a small bowl and slowly blend in the cream. Leave to stand while you prepare the pork and apple skewers.

2 Cut the pork fillet into bite-size pieces and set aside until required.

3 Core the apples, then cut them into thick wedges. Toss the apple wedges in a little lemon juice – this will prevent any discoloration. Cut the lemon into slices.

4 Thread the pork, apple and lemon slices alternately on to 4 skewers.

5 Mix together the mustards, fruit juice and oil. Brush the mixture over the kebabs (kabobs) and barbecue (grill) over hot coals for 10–15 minutes, turning and basting frequently with the mustard marinade.

6 Transfer the kebabs (kabobs) to warm serving plates and spoon over a little of the mustard sauce. Serve with fresh, crusty brown bread.

COOK'S TIP

There are many varieties of mustard available, including English mustard, which is very hot, Dijon, which is milder, and wholegrain mustard, which contains whole mustard seeds. Mustards flavoured with other ingredients, such as honey or chilli, are also available. It is well worth keeping some in the storecupboard.

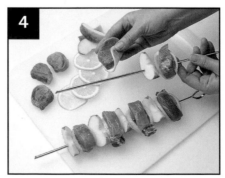

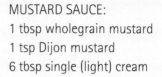

Pork Ribs with Plum Sauce

Pork ribs are always very popular at barbecues (grills), and you can flavour them with a number of spicy bastes. This slightly sweet version has a delicious oriental flavour.

Serves 4-6

INGREDIENTS

900 g/2 lb pork spare ribs
2 tbsp sunflower oil
1 tsp sesame oil
2 cloves garlic, crushed

2.5 cm/1 inch piece root (fresh) ginger, grated
150 ml/5 fl oz/^{2}/$_3$ cup plum sauce
2 tbsp dry sherry
2 tbsp Hoisin sauce

2 tbsp soy sauce
4-6 spring onions (scallions), to garnish (optional)

1 To prepare the garnish, trim the spring onions (scallions) to about 7.5 cm/3 inches long. Slice both ends into thin strips, leaving the onion intact in the centre.

2 Put the spring onions (scallions) into a bowl of iced water for at least 30 minutes until the ends start to curl up. Leave them in the water and set aside until required.

3 If you buy the spare ribs in a single piece, cut them into individual ribs. Bring a large pan of water to the boil and add the ribs. Cook for 5 minutes, then drain thoroughly.

4 Heat the oils together in a pan, add the garlic and ginger and cook gently for 1–2 minutes to bring out the flavour. Stir in the plum sauce, sherry, Hoisin sauce and soy sauce and heat through.

5 Brush the sauce over the pork ribs. Barbecue (grill) over hot coals for 5–10 minutes, then move the ribs to a cooler part of the barbecue (grill). Barbecue (grill) for a further 15–20 minutes, basting with the remaining sauce. Garnish with the spring onion (scallion) brushes, if using, and serve hot.

COOK'S TIP

Par-cooking the ribs in boiling water removes excess fat, which helps prevent the ribs from splitting during cooking. Do not be put off by the large quantity – there is only a little meat on each, but they are quite cheap to buy.

Fruity Pork Skewers

Prunes and apricots bring colour and flavour to these tasty pork kebabs (kabobs).

Makes 4

INGREDIENTS

4 boneless pork loin steaks
8 ready-to-eat prunes
8 ready-to-eat dried apricots
4 bay leaves

slices of orange and lemon, to garnish

MARINADE:
4 tbsp orange juice
2 tbsp olive oil
1 tsp ground bay leaves
salt and pepper

1 Trim the visible fat from the pork and cut the meat into evenly-sized chunks.

2 Place the pork in a shallow, non-metallic dish and add the prunes and apricots.

3 To make the marinade, mix together the orange juice, oil, bay leaves and salt and pepper to taste in a bowl.

4 Pour the marinade over the pork and fruit and toss until well coated. Leave to marinate in the refrigerator for at least 1 hour or preferably overnight.

5 Soak 4 wooden skewers in cold water to prevent them from catching alight on the barbecue (grill).

6 Remove the pork and fruit from the marinade, using a perforated spoon, reserving the marinade for basting. Thread the pork and fruit on to the skewers, alternating with the bay leaves.

7 Barbecue (grill) the skewers on an oiled rack over medium hot coals for 10–15 minutes, turning and frequently basting with the reserved marinade, or until the pork is cooked through.

8 Transfer the pork and fruit skewers to warm serving plates. Garnish with slices of orange and lemon and serve hot.

COOK'S TIP

Pork should always be thoroughly cooked through, but take care not to overcook it as the meat can become rather dry. Always add oil to a marinade for pork. If the meat is cooking too quickly, raise the rack or move to a cooler part of the barbecue (grill).

Spicy Pork Ribs

There are many ways of serving barbecued ribs.
This spicy sauce is based on a traditional American recipe.

Serves 4–6

INGREDIENTS

900 g/2 lb pork spare ribs
150 ml/5 fl oz/^{2}/$_3$ cup passata (sieved
  tomatoes)
2 tbsp red wine vinegar

2 tbsp dark muscovado sugar
1 clove garlic, crushed
1 tsp dried thyme
^{1}/$_2$ tsp dried rosemary

1 tsp chilli sauce
red chillies, to garnish (optional)
mixed salad leaves, to serve

1 If you buy the spare ribs in a single piece, carefully cut them into individual ribs using a very sharp knife.

2 Bring a large pan of water to the boil and add the ribs. Cook the ribs for 10 minutes, then drain them thoroughly. Place the ribs in a large, shallow, non-metallic dish.

3 To make the spicy sauce, combine the passata (sieved tomatoes), red wine vinegar, sugar, garlic, dried thyme, dried rosemary and chilli sauce in a bowl until well blended.

4 Pour the sauce over the pork ribs and toss to coat on all sides. Leave to marinate for 1 hour.

5 Remove the ribs from the sauce, reserving the sauce for basting. Barbecue (grill) the ribs over hot coals for 5–10 minutes, then move them to a cooler part of the barbecue (grill). Cook for a further 15–20 minutes, turning and basting frequently with the remaining sauce.

6 Transfer the ribs to warm serving plates and garnish with the red chillies (if using). Serve with the mixed salad leaves.

COOK'S TIP

For authentic American-style ribs make sure you buy pork spare ribs and not spare rib chops. Pork spare ribs are often sold cut into individual ribs, but it is quite easy to cut between the ribs with a sharp knife if you cannot buy them already separated.

Ham & Pineapple Kebabs (Kabobs)

This traditional combination of flavours always works well on the barbecue (grill).

Makes 4

INGREDIENTS

450 g/1 lb thick ham steak
425 g/15 oz can pineapple pieces, in natural juice
225 g/8 oz firm Brie, chilled

2 tbsp sunflower oil
1 clove garlic, crushed
1 tbsp lemon juice
$1/2$ tsp ground nutmeg

$1/4$ tsp ground cloves
pepper
cooked rice, to serve

1 Cut the ham into evenly-sized chunks.

2 Place the ham in a pan of boiling water and simmer for 5 minutes.

3 Drain the pineapple pieces and reserve 3 tbsp of the juice. Cut the chilled cheese into large chunks.

4 To make the baste, combine the pineapple juice, oil, garlic, lemon juice, nutmeg, cloves and pepper to taste in a small screw-top jar and shake until well combined. Set aside until required.

5 Remove the ham from the pan with a perforated spoon. Thread the ham on to skewers, alternating with the pineapple and cheese pieces.

6 Barbecue (grill) the kebabs (kabobs) over warm coals, turning and basting frequently with the oil and pineapple juice mixture, for 2–4 minutes on each side. Barbecue (grill) the kebabs (kabobs) until the pineapple and ham are hot and the cheese is just beginning to melt.

7 Serve the kebabs (kabobs) on a bed of cooked rice.

COOK'S TIP

Cook the skewers on the barbecue (grill) just long enough to reheat the gammon and to warm the pineapple. Take care not to overcook the kebabs (kabobs) or you will end up with a gooey mess – the cheese should only just begin to melt.

VARIATION

Add cubes of a hard cheese, such as Emmental or Jarlsburg, instead of the Brie, if you prefer.

Honey-glazed Pork Chops

The addition of freshly grated ginger gives a delicious tang to the honey-flavoured glaze.

Serves 4

INGREDIENTS

4 lean pork loin chops
4 tbsp clear honey
1 tbsp dry sherry

4 tbsp orange juice
2 tbsp olive oil
2.5 cm/1 inch piece root (fresh) ginger, grated

salt and pepper

1 Season the pork chops with salt and pepper to taste. Set aside while you make the glaze.

2 To make the glaze, place the honey, sherry, orange juice, oil and ginger in a small pan and heat gently, stirring continuously, until all of the ingredients are well blended.

3 Barbecue (grill) the chops on an oiled rack over hot coals for about 5 minutes on each side.

4 Brush the chops with the glaze and barbecue (grill) for a further 2–4 minutes on each side, basting frequently with the glaze.

5 Transfer the chops to warm serving plates and serve hot.

VARIATION

This recipe works equally well with lamb chops and with chicken portions, such as thighs or drumsticks. Barbecue (grill) the meat in exactly the same way as in this recipe, basting frequently with the honey glaze – the result will be just as delicious!

COOK'S TIP

To give the recipe a little more punch, stir ½ teaspoon of chilli sauce or 1 tablespoon of wholegrain mustard into the basting glaze.

Sausages with Barbecue Sauce

Although there is much more to barbecues (grills) than sausages, they can make a welcome appearance from time to time. This delicious sauce is a wonderful excuse for including them again.

Serves 4

INGREDIENTS

2 tbsp sunflower oil
1 large onion, chopped
2 cloves garlic, chopped
225 g/8 oz can chopped tomatoes
1 tbsp Worcestershire sauce

2 tbsp brown fruity sauce
2 tbsp light muscovado sugar
4 tbsp white wine vinegar
1/2 tsp mild chilli powder
1/4 tsp mustard powder

dash of Tabasco sauce
450 g/1 lb sausages
salt and pepper
bread finger rolls, to serve

1 To make the sauce, heat the oil in a small pan and fry the onion and garlic for 4–5 minutes until softened and just beginning to brown.

2 Add the tomatoes, Worcestershire sauce, brown fruity sauce, sugar, wine vinegar, chilli powder, mustard powder, Tabasco sauce and salt and pepper to taste to the pan and bring to the boil.

3 Reduce the heat and simmer gently for 10–15 minutes until the sauce begins to thicken slightly. Stir occasionally so that the sauce does not burn and stick to the bottom of the pan. Set aside and keep warm until required.

4 Barbecue (grill) the sausages over hot coals for 10–15 minutes, turning frequently. Do not prick them with a fork or the juices and fat will run out and cause the barbecue (grill) to flare.

5 Insert the sausages into the bread rolls and serve with the barbecue sauce.

COOK'S TIP

Choose any well-flavoured sausages for this recipe. Lincolnshire sausages are a good choice as are Cumberland sausages, which are also available in a coil (secure the coil with skewers so that it does not unravel as it cooks). Venison sausages have a good, gamey flavour and taste wonderful cooked on the barbecue (grill). Black pudding can be barbecued (grilled) if it is cut into thick slices, as can the more strongly flavoured continental sausages.

Tangy Pork Fillet

Barbecued (grilled) in a parcel of kitchen foil, these tasty pork fillets are served with a tangy orange sauce.

Serves 4

INGREDIENTS

400 g/14 oz pork fillet
3 tbsp orange marmalade
grated rind and juice of 1 orange
1 tbsp white wine vinegar
dash of Tabasco sauce
salt and pepper

SAUCE:
1 tbsp olive oil
1 small onion, chopped
1 small green (bell) pepper, deseeded
  and thinly sliced
1 tbsp cornflour (cornstarch)

150 ml/5 fl oz/^{2}/$_3$ cup orange juice

TO SERVE:
cooked rice
mixed salad leaves

1 Place a large piece of double thickness foil in a shallow dish. Put the pork fillet in the centre of the foil and season.

2 Heat the marmalade, orange rind and juice, vinegar and Tabasco sauce in a small pan, stirring until the marmalade melts and the ingredients combine.

3 Pour the mixture over the pork and wrap the meat in foil, making sure that the parcel is well sealed so that the juices cannot run out. Place over hot coals and barbecue (grill) for about 25 minutes, turning the parcel occasionally.

4 To make the sauce, heat the oil and cook the onion for 2–3 minutes until softened. Add the (bell) pepper and cook for 3–4 minutes until it is just tender.

5 Remove the pork from the kitchen foil and place on to the rack. Pour the cooking juices into the pan containing the sauce.

6 Barbecue (grill) the pork for a further 10–20 minutes, turning, until cooked through and golden on the outside.

7 In a small bowl, mix the cornflour (cornstarch) with a little orange juice to form a paste. Add to the sauce with the remaining cooking juices. Cook, stirring, until the sauce thickens.

8 Cut the pork into slices and transfer to serving plates. Spoon over the sauce and serve.

Pork & Sage Kebabs (Kabobs)

The pork mince mixture is shaped into meatballs and threaded on to skewers.
They have a delicious, slightly sweet flavour that is popular with children.

Makes 12

INGREDIENTS

450 g/1 lb pork mince
25 g/1 oz fresh breadcrumbs
1 small onion, chopped very finely
1 tbsp fresh sage, chopped
2 tbsp apple sauce
1/4 tsp ground nutmeg

salt and pepper

BASTE:
3 tbsp olive oil
1 tbsp lemon juice

TO SERVE:
6 small pitta breads
mixed salad leaves
6 tbsp thick, natural yogurt

1 Place the mince in a mixing bowl together with the breadcrumbs, onion, sage, apple sauce, nutmeg and salt and pepper to taste. Mix until the ingredients are well combined.

2 Using your hands, shape the mixture into small balls, about the size of large marbles, and leave to chill in the refrigerator for at least 30 minutes.

3 Meanwhile, soak 12 small wooden skewers in cold water for at least 30 minutes. Thread the meatballs on to the skewers.

4 To make the baste, mix together the oil and lemon juice in a small bowl, whisking with a fork until it is well blended.

5 Barbecue (grill) the kebabs (kabobs) over hot coals for 8–10 minutes, turning and basting frequently with the lemon and oil mixture, until the meat is golden and cooked through.

6 Line the pitta breads with the salad leaves and spoon over some of the yogurt. Serve with the kebabs (kababs).

VARIATION

Save time by shaping the meat mixture into burgers. Leave to chill for at least 20 minutes, then barbecue (grill), basting with the oil and lemon mixture for 15 minutes, turning once. Serve in burger buns topped with a little apple sauce.

Steak & Kidney Kebabs (Kabobs)

A traditional English dish is transformed for the barbecue (grill).
Marinate the meat overnight if possible to enable the flavours to be fully absorbed.

Makes 4

INGREDIENTS

350 g/12 oz rump steak	150 ml/5 fl oz/$^{2}/_{3}$ cup brown ale (beer)	TO SERVE:
2 lamb's kidneys	8 button mushrooms	cooked rice
1 small onion, sliced	8 bay leaves	cherry tomatoes
$^{1}/_{2}$ tsp dried rosemary	4 tbsp sunflower oil	

1 Using a sharp knife, trim the steak and cut it into evenly-sized pieces.

2 Cut the kidneys in half and remove the skin. Snip out the core and cut each kidney half into half again.

3 Place the steak and kidney pieces in a shallow, non-metallic dish.

4 Add the onions and rosemary to the dish and pour over the beer. Cover and leave to marinate in the refrigerator for at least 4 hours or preferably overnight.

5 Remove the meat from the marinade, reserving 4 tbsp of the marinade for basting.

6 Thread the steak and kidney pieces on to the skewers, alternating with the mushrooms and the bay leaves.

7 Stir the oil into the reserved marinade.

8 Barbecue (grill) the kebabs (kabobs) over hot coals for 8–10 minutes, turning and basting with the reserved marinade. Take care not to overcook the kidneys or they will become tough.

9 Serve the kebabs (kabobs) on a bed of cooked rice and with a few cherry tomatoes.

COOK'S TIP

To save time on the day, prepare and marinate the kebabs (kabobs) a day in advance. Place them in a shallow dish and pour over the marinade. Turn the kebabs (kabobs) occasionally to make sure that they are completely coated in the marinade.

Mixed Grill Skewers

If you like a mixed grill, this dish is for you. The addition of barbecued (grilled) tomatoes and mushrooms makes this a complete meal.

Serves 4

INGREDIENTS

225 g/8 oz lamb neck fillet
4 lamb's kidneys
4 thick sausages
8 rashers rindless, streaky bacon

BASTE:
4 tbsp olive oil
2 tbsp lemon juice
1 tbsp fresh mixed herbs, chopped

TO SERVE:
4 flat mushrooms
2 beef steak tomatoes

1 Cut the lamb fillet into evenly-sized pieces. Skin and core the kidneys and cut each kidney into 4 pieces.

2 Twist the sausages in the centre and cut each sausage in half.

3 Stretch out the bacon rashers with the back of a knife.

4 Either wrap the bacon around the sausages or simply roll up the rashers on their own. Thread the lamb, sausage, bacon and kidneys on to skewers.

5 To make the baste, mix together the oil, lemon juice and mixed herbs and leave to stand until required.

6 Barbecue (grill) the kebabs (kababs) over hot coals, turning and basting frequently, for 8–10 minutes.

7 Cut the tomatoes and mushrooms into large chunks and thread them on to separate skewers. Barbecue (grill) the tomato and mushroom skewers next to the meat for 5 minutes, turning and basting frequently.

8 Transfer the meat skewers to serving plates and serve hot with the tomato and mushroom skewers.

COOK'S TIP

All the elements of this dish can be cooked directly on the barbecue (grill). However, threading them on to skewers makes them quicker and less fiddly to turn and baste.

Liver & Onion Kebabs (Kabobs)

Liver is full of iron, making this dish nutritious as well as flavoursome.

Makes 4

INGREDIENTS

350 g/12 oz lamb's liver
2 tbsp seasoned plain (all-purpose)
   flour
1/2 tsp dried mixed herbs

125 g/4 1/2 oz rindless streaky bacon
2 medium onions
75 g/2 3/4 oz butter
2 tsp balsamic vinegar

TO SERVE:
mixed salad leaves
tomato quarters

1 Cut the liver into bite-sized pieces. Mix the flour with the dried herbs and toss the liver in the seasoned flour.

2 Stretch out the bacon rashers with the back of a knife. Cut each rasher in half and wrap the bacon around half of the liver pieces.

3 Thread the plain liver pieces on to skewers, alternating with the bacon-wrapped liver pieces.

4 Cut the onions into rings and thread over the kebabs (kabobs). Finely chop the onion

rings that are too small to thread over the kebabs (kabobs).

5 Heat the butter in a small pan and sauté the chopped onions for about 5 minutes until softened. Stir in the vinegar.

6 Brush the butter mixture over the kebabs (kabobs) and barbecue (grill) over hot coals for 8–10 minutes, basting occasionally with the butter mixture, until the liver is just cooked but is still a little pink inside.

7 Transfer the kebabs (kabobs) to serving plates. Serve with mixed salad leaves and tomatoes.

COOK'S TIP

Choose thick slices of liver to give good-sized pieces. Use bacon to hold 2–3 pieces of thinner liver together if necessary.

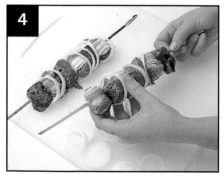

Vegetables & Salads

You will find all the barbecue (grill) extras you will need in this chapter, from more-ish nibbles and stylish starters to vegetarian main courses and colourful side dishes.

Vegetarians need never feel left out as many vegetables cook well on the barbecue (grill), and they taste delicious. Try the Colourful Vegetable Kebabs (Kabobs), the Nutty Rice Burgers, the Vegetarian Sausages or the delicious Marinated Tofu (Bean Curd) Kebabs (Kabobs). Cook vegetables whole, sliced on skewers or in parcels for main dishes or as tasty side dishes.

Keep your diners happy while they wait for the main course with some tasty nibbles, such as Crispy Potato Skins, Garlic Bread or Mediterranean Bruschetta, while Stuffed Mushrooms and Stuffed Tomatoes make ideal starters for your vegetarian guests.

If you need inspiration for salads to accompany your barbecued (grilled) food, look no further. All the salads in this chapter go well with barbecued (grilled) dishes, and many make ideal starters. Pear & Roquefort Salad and Artichoke & Parma Ham (Prosciutto) Salad are stylish starters that can be prepared well in advance.

Marinated Tofu (Bean Curd) Skewers

Tofu (bean curd) is full of protein, vitamins and minerals, and although it is rather bland on its own, it develops a fabulous flavour when it is marinated in garlic and herbs.

Serves 4

INGREDIENTS

350 g/12 oz tofu (bean curd)
1 red (bell) pepper
1 yellow (bell) pepper
2 courgettes (zucchini)
8 button mushrooms

slices of lemon, to garnish

MARINADE:
grated rind and juice of $^1/_2$ lemon
1 clove garlic, crushed

$^1/_2$ tsp fresh rosemary, chopped
$^1/_2$ tsp chopped, fresh thyme
1 tbsp walnut oil

1 To make the marinade, combine the lemon rind and juice, garlic, rosemary, thyme and oil in a shallow dish.

2 Drain the tofu (bean curd), pat it dry on kitchen paper and cut it into squares. Add to the marinade and toss to coat. Leave to marinate for 20–30 minutes.

3 Meanwhile, deseed and cut the (bell) peppers into 2.5 cm/1 inch pieces. Blanch in boiling water for 4 minutes, refresh in cold water and drain.

4 Using a canelle knife (or potato peeler), remove strips of peel from the courgettes (zucchini). Cut the courgette (zucchini) into 2.5 cm/1 inch chunks.

5 Remove the tofu (bean curd) from the marinade, reserving the liquid for basting. Thread the tofu (bean curd) on to 8 skewers, alternating with the (bell) peppers, courgette (zucchini) and button mushrooms.

6 Barbecue (grill) the skewers over medium hot coals for

about 6 minutes, turning and basting with the marinade.

7 Transfer the skewers to warm serving plates, garnish with slices of lemon and serve.

VARIATION

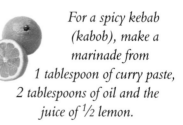

For a spicy kebab (kabob), make a marinade from 1 tablespoon of curry paste, 2 tablespoons of oil and the juice of $^1/_2$ lemon.

Crispy Potato Skins

Use the potato flesh in this recipe for another meal, so make slightly more than you think you need. They make a delicious and more-ish starter.

Serves 4-6

INGREDIENTS

8 small baking potatoes, scrubbed
50 g/1³/₄ oz butter, melted
salt and pepper

OPTIONAL TOPPING:
6 spring onions (scallions), sliced
50 g/1 ³/₄ oz salami, cut into thin
strips

50 g/1³/₄ oz grated gruyère cheese

1 Preheat the oven to 200°C/400°F/Gas Mark 6. Prick the potatoes with a fork and bake for 1 hour or until tender. Alternatively, cook in a microwave on High for 12–15 minutes.

2 Cut the potatoes in half and scoop out the flesh, leaving about 5 mm/¼ inch potato flesh lining the skin.

3 Brush the insides of the potato with melted butter.

4 Place the skins, cut-side down, over medium hot coals and barbecue (grill) for 10–15 minutes. Turn the potato skins over and barbecue (grill) for a further 5 minutes or until they are crispy. Take care that they do not burn.

5 Season the potato skins with salt and pepper to taste and serve while they are still warm.

6 If wished, the skins can filled with a variety of toppings. Barbecue (grill) the potato skins as above for about 10 minutes, then turn cut-side up and sprinkle with slices of spring onion (scallion), grated cheese and chopped salami. Barbecue (grill) for a further 5 minutes until the cheese begins to melt. Serve hot.

COOK'S TIP

Potato skins can be served on their own but they are delicious served with a dip. Try a spicy tomato or hummus dip.

Spicy Sweet Potato Slices

Serve these as an accompaniment to other barbecue (grill) dishes or with a spicy dip as nibbles. They are ideal at parties if you need to keep guests happy while the main dishes are being cooked.

Serves 4

INGREDIENTS

450 g/1 lb sweet potatoes
2 tbsp sunflower oil

1 tsp chilli sauce

salt and pepper

1 Bring a large pan of water to the boil, add the sweet potatoes and par-boil them for 10 minutes. Drain thoroughly and transfer to a chopping board.

2 Peel the potatoes and cut them into thick slices.

3 Mix together the oil, chilli sauce and salt and pepper to taste in a small bowl.

4 Brush the spicy mixture liberally over one side of the potatoes. Place the potatoes, oil side down, over medium hot coals and barbecue (grill) for 5–6 minutes.

5 Lightly brush the tops of the potatoes with the oil, turn them over and barbecue (grill) for a further 5 minutes or until crisp and golden.

6 Transfer the potatoes to a warm serving dish and serve at once.

COOK'S TIP

Although it is a vegetable the sweet potato is used in both sweet and savoury dishes. It is very versatile and can be boiled, roasted, fried, or cooked as here over a barbecue (grill).

VARIATION

For a simple spicy dip combine 150 ml/5 fl oz/²/3 cup sour cream with 1/2 teaspoon of sugar, 1/2 teaspoon of Dijon mustard and salt and pepper to taste. Leave to chill until required.

Barbecued Garlic Potato Wedges

Serve this tasty potato dish with grilled (broiled) meat or fish.

Serves 4

INGREDIENTS

3 large baking potatoes, scrubbed
4 tbsp olive oil
25 g/1 oz butter

2 garlic cloves, chopped
1 tbsp chopped, fresh rosemary
1 tbsp chopped, fresh parsley

1 tbsp chopped, fresh thyme
salt and pepper

1 Bring a large pan of water to the boil, add the potatoes and par-boil them for 10 minutes. Drain the potatoes, refresh under cold water and drain them again thoroughly.

2 Transfer the potatoes to a chopping board. When the potatoes are cold enough to handle, cut them into thick wedges, but do not remove the skins.

3 Heat the oil and butter in a small pan together with the garlic. Cook gently until the garlic begins to brown, then remove the pan from the heat.

4 Stir the herbs and salt and pepper to taste into the mixture in the pan.

5 Brush the herb mixture all over the potatoes.

6 Barbecue (grill) the potatoes over hot coals for 10–15 minutes, brushing liberally with any of the remaining herb and butter mixture, or until the potatoes are just tender.

7 Transfer the barbecued garlic potatoes to a warm serving plate and serve as a starter or as a side dish.

COOK'S TIP

You may find it easier to barbecue (grill) these potatoes in a hinged rack or in a specially designed barbecue (grill) roasting tray.

Vegetarian Sausages

The deliciously cheesy flavour is certain to make these sausages a hit with vegetarians who have no need to feel left out when it comes to tasty barbecued (grilled) food.

Makes 8

INGREDIENTS

1 tbsp sunflower oil
1 small onion, chopped finely
50 g/1³/4 oz mushrooms, chopped finely
1/2 red (bell) pepper, deseeded and chopped finely

400 g/14 oz can cannolini beans, rinsed and drained
100 g/3¹/2 oz fresh breadcrumbs
100 g/3¹/2 oz Cheddar cheese, grated
1 tsp dried mixed herbs
1 egg yolk

seasoned plain (all-purpose) flour
oil, to baste

TO SERVE:
bread rolls
slices of fried onion

1 Heat the oil in a saucepan and fry the prepared onion, mushrooms and (bell) peppers until softened.

2 Mash the cannolini beans in a large mixing bowl. Add the onion, mushroom and (bell) pepper mixture, the breadcrumbs, cheese, herbs and egg yolk, and mix together well.

3 Press the mixture together with your fingers and shape into 8 sausages.

4 Roll each sausage in the seasoned flour. Leave to chill in the refrigerator for at least 30 minutes.

5 Barbecue (grill) the sausages on a sheet of oiled foil set over medium coals for 15–20 minutes, turning and basting frequently with oil, until golden.

6 Split a bread roll down the middle and insert a layer of fried onions. Place the sausage in the roll and serve.

COOK'S TIP

Take care not to break the sausages when you turning them over. If you have a hinged rack, oil this and place the sausages inside, turning and oiling frequently. Look out for racks that are especially designed for barbecueing (grilling) sausages.

Nutty Rice Burgers

Serve these burgers in toasted sesame seed baps. If you wish, add a slice of cheese to top the burger at the end of cooking.

Makes 6

INGREDIENTS

1 tbsp sunflower oil
1 small onion, chopped finely
100 g/3^1/$_2$ oz mushrooms, chopped finely
350 g/12 oz/8 cups cooked brown rice
100 g/3^1/$_2$ oz breadcrumbs

75 g/2^3/$_4$ oz walnuts, chopped
1 egg
2 tbsp brown fruity sauce
dash of Tabasco sauce
salt and pepper
oil, to baste
6 individual cheese slices (optional)

TO SERVE:
6 sesame seed baps
slices of onion
slices of tomato
green salad leaves

1 Heat the oil in a large saucepan and fry the onions for 3–4 minutes until they just begin to soften. Add the mushrooms and cook for a further 2 minutes.

2 Remove the pan from the heat and mix the rice, breadcrumbs, walnuts, egg and sauces into the vegetables. Season with salt and pepper and mix well.

3 Shape the mixture into 6 burgers, pressing the mixture together with your fingers. Leave to chill in the refrigerator for at least 30 minutes.

4 Barbecue (grill) the burgers on an oiled rack over medium coals for 5–6 minutes on each side, turning once and frequently basting with oil.

5 If liked, top the burgers with a slice of cheese 2 minutes before the end of the cooking time. Barbecue (grill) the onion and tomato slices.

6 Toast the sesame seed baps at the side of the barbecue. Serve the burgers in the baps, together with the barbecued (grilled) onions and tomatoes.

COOK'S TIP

It is quicker and more economical to use leftover rice to make these burgers. However, if you are cooking the rice for this dish you will need to use 175 g/6 oz/1 cup uncooked rice.

Aubergine (Eggplant) & Mozzarella Sandwiches

Serve these sandwiches as a vegetarian main course for two or as a side dish to accompany other barbecued (grilled) foods.

Serves 2

INGREDIENTS

1 large aubergine (eggplant)
1 tbsp lemon juice
3 tbsp olive oil

125 g/4 ^{1}/2 oz grated Mozzarella cheese
2 sun-dried tomatoes, chopped
salt and pepper

TO SERVE:
Italian bread
mixed salad leaves
slices of tomato

1 Slice the aubergine (eggplant) into thin rounds.

2 Combine the lemon juice and olive oil in a small bowl and season the mixture with salt and pepper to taste.

3 Brush the aubergine (eggplant) slices with the oil and lemon juice mixture and barbecue (grill) over medium hot coals for 2–3 minutes, without turning, until they are golden on the under side.

4 Turn half of the aubergine (eggplant) slices over and sprinkle with cheese and chopped sun-dried tomatoes.

5 Place the remaining aubergine (eggplant) slices on top of the cheese and tomatoes, turning them so that the pale side is uppermost.

6 Barbecue (grill) for 1–2 minutes, then carefully turn the whole sandwich over and barbecue (grill) for 1–2 minutes. Baste with the oil mixture.

7 Serve with Italian bread, mixed salad leaves and a few slices of tomato.

VARIATION

Try Feta cheese instead of Mozzarella but omit the salt from the basting oil because Feta is quite salty. A creamy goat's cheese would be equally delicious.

Char-grilled Aubergine (Eggplant)

The wonderful flavour and texture of char-grilled aubergines (eggplants) is hard to beat.
Serve plain as a simple vegetable dish, but for a tasty starter or vegetarian dish,
serve it accompanied with pesto or minty cucumber sauce.

Serves 4

INGREDIENTS

1 large aubergine (eggplant)
3 tbsp olive oil
1 tsp sesame oil
salt and pepper

PESTO:
1 clove garlic
25 g/1 oz pine nuts
15 g/^{1}/$_2$ oz fresh basil leaves
2 tbsp Parmesan cheese
6 tbsp olive oil
salt and pepper

CUCUMBER SAUCE:
150 g/5^1/$_2$ oz natural yogurt
5 cm/2 inch cucumber
^{1}/$_2$ tsp mint sauce

1 Remove the stalk from the aubergine (eggplant), then cut it lengthwise into 8 thin slices.

2 Lay the slices on a plate or board and sprinkle them liberally with salt to remove the bitter juices. Leave to stand.

3 Meanwhile, prepare the baste. Combine the olive and sesame oils, season with pepper and set aside.

4 To make the pesto, put the garlic, pine nuts, basil and cheese in a food processor until finely chopped. With the machine running, gradually add the oil in a thin stream. Season to taste.

5 To make the minty cucumber sauce, place the yogurt in a mixing bowl. Remove the seeds from the cucumber and dice the flesh finely. Stir into the yogurt with the mint sauce.

6 Rinse the aubergine (eggplant) slices and pat them dry on absorbent kitchen paper. Baste with the oil mixture and barbecue (grill) over hot coals for about 10 minutes, turning once. The aubergine (eggplant) should be golden and tender.

7 Transfer the aubergine (eggplant) slices to serving plates and serve with either the cucumber sauce or the pesto.

Stuffed Tomatoes

Theses barbecued (grilled) tomato cups are filled with a delicious
Greek-style combination of herbs, nuts and raisins.

Makes 8

INGREDIENTS

4 beefsteak tomatoes
300 g/10^1/$_2$ oz /4^1/$_2$ cups cooked rice
8 spring onions (scallions), chopped

3 tbsp chopped, fresh mint
2 tbsp chopped, fresh parsley
3 tbsp pine nuts

3 tbsp raisins
2 tsp olive oil
salt and pepper

1 Cut the tomatoes in half, then scoop out the seeds and discard.

2 Stand the tomatoes upside down on absorbent kitchen paper for a few moments in order for the juices to drain out.

3 Turn the tomatoes the right way up and sprinkle the insides with salt and pepper.

4 Mix together the rice, spring onions (scallions), mint, parsley, pine nuts and raisins. Spoon the mixture into the tomato cups.

5 Drizzle over a little olive oil, then barbecue (grill) the tomatoes on an oiled rack over medium hot coals for about 10 minutes until they are tender.

6 Transfer the tomatoes to serving plates and serve immediately.

VARIATION

Cook regular tomatoes, cut in half, brushed with oil and seasoned with salt and pepper, barbecueing (grilling) them cut-side down first.

COOK'S TIP

Tomatoes are a popular barbecue (grill) vegetable and can be quickly cooked. Try grilling (broiling) slices of beefsteak tomato and slices of onion brushed with a little oil and topped with sprigs of fresh herbs. In addition, cherry tomatoes can be threaded on to skewers and barbecued (grilled) for 5–10 minutes until hot.

Colourful Vegetable Kebabs (Kabobs)

Brighten up a barbecue (grill) meal with these colourful kebabs (kabobs).
They are basted with a flavoured oil.

Serves 4

INGREDIENTS

1 red (bell) pepper, deseeded
1 yellow (bell) pepper, deseeded
1 green (bell) pepper, deseeded
1 small onion

8 cherry tomatoes
100 g/3½ oz wild mushrooms

SEASONED OIL:
6 tbsp olive oil
1 clove garlic, crushed
½ tsp mixed dried herbs or herbes
de Provence

1 Cut the (bell) peppers into 2.5 cm/1 inch pieces.

2 Peel the onion and cut it into wedges, leaving the root end just intact to help keep the wedges together.

3 Thread the (bell) peppers, onion wedges, tomatoes and mushrooms on to skewers, alternating the colours of the (bell) peppers.

4 To make the seasoned oil, mix together the oil, garlic and herbs in a a small bowl. Brush the mixture liberally over the kebabs (kabobs).

5 Barbecue (grill) the kebabs (kabobs) over medium hot coals for 10–15 minutes, brushing with more of the seasoned oil and turning the skewers frequently.

6 Transfer the vegetable kebabs (kabobs) to warm serving plates. Serve the kebabs (kabobs) with walnut sauce (see Cook's Tip, right), if you wish.

COOK'S TIP

These kebabs (kabobs) are delicious when accompanied with a walnut sauce. To make the sauce, process 125 g/4 ½ oz walnuts in a food processor until they form a smooth paste. With the machine running, add 150 ml/5 fl oz/⅔ cup double (heavy) cream and 1 tablespoon of olive oil. Season to taste. Alternatively, finely chop the walnuts then pound them in a pestle and mortar to form a paste. Mix with the cream and oil, and season.

Char-grilled Mixed Vegetables

This combination of barbecued (grilled) vegetables is a perfect accompaniment for barbecued (grilled) meat or fish.

Serves 4-6

INGREDIENTS

8 baby aubergines (eggplant)
4 courgettes (zucchini)
2 red onions
4 tomatoes
salt and pepper

1 tsp balsamic vinegar, to serve

BASTE:
75 g/2³/₄ oz butter
2 tsp walnut oil

2 cloves garlic, chopped
4 tbsp dry white wine or cider

1 To prepare the vegetables, cut the aubergines (eggplant) in half. Trim and cut the courgettes (zucchini) in half lengthwise. Thickly slice the onion and halve the tomatoes.

2 Season all of the vegetables with salt and pepper to taste.

3 To make the baste, melt the butter with the oil in a saucepan. Add the garlic and cook gently for 1–2 minutes. Remove the pan from the heat and stir in the wine or cider.

4 Add the vegetables to the pan and toss them in the baste mixture. You may need to do this in several batches to ensure that all of the vegetables are coated evenly with the baste mixture.

5 Remove the vegetables from the baste mixture, reserving any excess baste. Place the vegetables on an oiled rack over medium hot coals. Barbecue (grill) the vegetables for 15–20 minutes, basting with the reserved baste mixture and turning once or twice during cooking.

6 Transfer the vegetables to warm serving plates and serve sprinkled with balsamic vinegar.

COOK'S TIP

Use a long-handled brush for basting food on the barbecue (grill).

Stuffed Mushrooms

Serve these mushrooms as a side vegetable or as an appetizer. For non-vegetarians, replace the cheese with chopped chorizo sausage.

Makes 12

INGREDIENTS

12 open-cap mushrooms
4 spring onions (scallions), chopped
4 tsp olive oil

100 g/3$^1/_2$ oz fresh brown
  breadcrumbs
1 tsp fresh oregano, chopped

100 g/3$^1/_2$ oz Feta cheese or chorizo
  sausage

1 Remove the stalks from the mushrooms and chop the stalks finely.

2 Sauté the mushroom stalks and spring onions (scallions) in half of the oil.

3 In a large bowl, mix together the mushroom stalks and spring onions (scallions). Add the breadcrumbs and oregano to the mushrooms and spring onions (scallions), mix and set aside.

4 If using Feta, crumble the cheese into small pieces in a small bowl.

5 If you are using chorizo sausage, remove the skin and chop the flesh finely.

6 Add the cheese or chorizo to the breadcrumb mixture and mix well.

7 Spoon the stuffing mixture into the mushroom caps.

8 Drizzle the oil over the mushrooms. Barbecue (grill) on an oiled rack over medium hot coals for 8–10 minutes.

9 Transfer the mushrooms to serving plates and serve hot.

COOK'S TIP

If only small mushrooms are available, place a sheet of oiled kitchen foil on top of the barbecue (grill) rack and cook the mushrooms on this. This will stop the smaller mushrooms from cooking too quickly and burning, and it will also prevent any excess stuffing mixture from dropping on to the coals during cooking.

Corn-on-the-cob

There are a number of ways of cooking corn-on-the-cob on the barbecue (grill).
Leaving on the husks protects the tender corn niblets.

Serves 4

INGREDIENTS

4 cobs of sweetcorn, with husks
100 g/3^{1}/$_{2}$ oz butter
1 tbsp chopped, fresh parsley

1 tsp chopped, fresh chives
1 tsp chopped, fresh thyme
rind of 1 lemon, grated

salt and pepper

1 To prepare the cobs of sweetcorn, peel back the husks and remove the silken hairs.

2 Fold back the husks and secure them in place with string if necessary.

3 Blanch the cobs of sweetcorn in a large saucepan of boiling water for about 5 minutes. Remove the cobs with a perforated spoon and drain thoroughly.

4 Barbecue (grill) the cobs over medium hot coals for 20–30 minutes, turning frequently.

5 Meanwhile, soften the butter and beat in the parsley, chives, thyme, lemon rind and salt and pepper to taste.

6 Transfer the cobs of sweetcorn to serving plates, remove the string and pull back the husks. Serve with a generous portion of herb butter.

COOK'S TIP

Cooking the cobs with the husk still on allows them to retain more moisture during barbecueing (grilling) so they won't dry out.

COOK'S TIP

When you are buying fresh sweetcorn, look for plump, tightly packed kernels. If you are unable to get fresh cobs, cook frozen sweetcorn cobs on the barbecue (grill). Spread some of the herb butter on to a sheet of double thickness kitchen foil. Wrap the cobs in the foil and barbecue (grill) among the coals for 20–30 minutes.

Pumpkin Parcels with Chilli & Lime

This spicy side dish is perfect for a Hallowe'en or Bonfire Night barbecue (grill).

Serves 4

INGREDIENTS

700 g/1 lb 9oz pumpkin or squash
2 tbsp sunflower oil

25 g/1 oz butter
1/2 tsp chilli sauce

rind of 1 lime, grated
2 tsp lime juice

1 Halve the pumpkin or squash and scoop out the seeds. Rinse the seeds and reserve. Cut the pumpkin into thin wedges and peel.

2 Heat the oil and butter together in a large saucepan, stirring continuously until melted. Stir in the chilli sauce, lime rind and juice.

3 Add the pumpkin or squash and seeds to the pan and toss to coat on all sides in the flavoured butter.

4 Divide the mixture among 4 double thickness sheets of kitchen foil. Fold over the kitchen

foil to enclose the pumpkin or squash mixture completely.

5 Barbecue (grill) the foil parcels over hot coals for 15–25 minutes or until the pumpkin or squash is tender.

6 Transfer the foil parcels to warm serving plates. Open the parcels at the table and serve at once.

VARIATION

Add 2 teaspoons of curry paste to the oil instead of the lime and chilli. Use butternut squash when pumpkin is not available.

COOK'S TIP

Always take care when you handle chillies. It is a good idea to wear disposable gloves when you are slicing and deseeding them. Alternatively, rub a little oil over your fingers before you begin – the oil will help to prevent your skin absorbing the chilli juice. Wash your hands thoroughly afterwards.

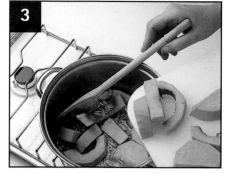

Garlic Bread

A perennial favourite, garlic bread is perfect with a range of barbecue (grill) meals.

Serves 6

INGREDIENTS

150 g/5¹/₂ oz butter, softened
3 cloves garlic, crushed

2 tbsp chopped, fresh parsley
pepper

1 large or 2 small sticks of French
bread

1 Mix together the butter, garlic and parsley in a bowl until well combined. Season to taste with pepper and mix well.

2 Cut the French bread into thick slices.

3 Spread the flavoured butter over one side of each slice and reassemble the loaf on a large sheet of thick kitchen foil.

4 Wrap the bread well and barbecue (grill) over hot coals for 10–15 minutes until the butter melts and the bread is piping hot.

5 Serve as an accompaniment to a wide range of dishes.

VARIATION

For a tasty variation, sprinkle a little grated Mozzarella cheese between each slice of bread. Reassemble the loaf and barbecue (grill) for 10–15 minutes, until the cheese has just melted.

COOK'S TIP

Some recipes suggest that you do not cut all the way through the bread when you slice it, but you will find it a lot easier to serve if you do. Simply keep the slices in order and reassemble once buttered.

COOK'S TIP

When garlic is cooked like this on a barbecue (grill), the sweetness of it comes to the fore. Garlic combines well with fresh, crusty white bread and the result tastes delicious.

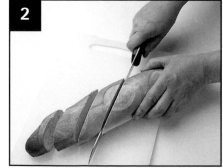

Mediterranean Bruschetta

This modern version of garlic bread originates from Italy. It is important to use a good quality olive oil for this recipe. Serve the bruschetta with kebabs (kabobs) or fish for a really summery taste.

Serves 4

INGREDIENTS

1 ciabatta loaf or small stick of French bread

1 plump clove garlic
extra virgin olive oil

fresh Parmesan cheese, grated (optional)

1 Slice the bread in half crossways and again lengthwise to give 4 portions.

2 Do not peel the garlic clove, but cut it in half.

3 Barbecue (grill) the bread over hot coals for a few minutes on both sides until golden brown.

4 Rub the garlic, cut side down, all over the toasted surface of the bread.

5 Drizzle the olive oil over the bread and serve hot as an accompaniment.

6 If using Parmesan cheese, sprinkle the cheese over the bread. Return the bread to the barbecue (grill), cut side up, for 1–2 minutes until the cheese just begins to melt. Serve hot.

COOK'S TIP

As ready-grated Parmesan quickly loses its pungency and 'bite', it is better to buy small quantities of the cheese in one piece and grate it yourself as needed. Tightly wrapped in cling film (plastic wrap) or foil, it will keep in the refrigerator for several months. Grate it just before using, for maximum flavour.

VARIATION

For a tasty appetizer, serve the bruschetta topped with chopped tomatoes mixed with a few chopped anchovies or olives.

COOK'S TIP

If you do not peel the garlic the smell will not transfer to your fingers.

Caesar Salad

This traditional American salad has a good robust flavour

Serves 6-8

INGREDIENTS

2 thick slices of white bread
2 tbsp sunflower oil
2 rashers streaky bacon

1 clove garlic
50 g/1³/₄ oz fresh Parmesan cheese
1 large cos (romaine) lettuce

DRESSING:
1 small egg
juice 1 lemon
6 tbsp olive oil
salt and white pepper

1 To make the croûtons, remove the crusts from the bread and discard. Cut the bread into small cubes. Heat the oil in a frying pan (skillet) and fry the bread cubes until golden-brown. Drain on absorbent kitchen paper.

2 Remove the rind from the bacon and discard. Chop the bacon and fry until crisp. Drain on absorbent kitchen paper.

3 Cut the garlic in half and rub all around the inside of a serving dish. This will give the salad just a hint of garlic.

4 Wash the lettuce, tear into bite-size pieces and place in the serving dish.

5 Using a potato peeler, shave peelings off the Parmesan.

6 To make the dressing, whisk the egg in a small bowl. Gradually whisk in the lemon juice and oil. Season with salt and pepper to taste.

7 Pour the salad dressing over the lettuce and toss to coat. Serve sprinkled with the croûtons, bacon and Parmesan shavings.

COOK'S TIP

Pregnant women, children and people with weak immune systems may wish to avoid eating recipes containing raw egg.

VARIATION

Use 6 chopped anchovies instead of the bacon, if you prefer.

Coleslaw

Always popular, home-made coleslaw tastes far superior to any that you can buy.

SERVES 10–12

INGREDIENTS

150 ml/5 fl oz/²/3 cup mayonnaise
150 ml/5 fl oz/²/3 cup low-fat natural yogurt

dash of Tabasco sauce
1 medium head white cabbage
4 carrots

1 green (bell) pepper
2 tbsp sunflower seeds
salt and pepper

1 To make the dressing, combine the mayonnaise, yogurt, Tabasco sauce and salt and pepper to taste in a small bowl. Leave to chill in the refrigerator until required.

2 Cut the cabbage in half and then into quarters. Remove and discard the tough centre stalk. Shred the cabbage leaves finely. Wash the leaves and dry them thoroughly.

3 Peel the carrot and shred in a food processor or on a mandolin. Alternatively, coarsely grate the carrot.

4 Quarter and deseed the (bell) pepper and cut the flesh into thin strips.

5 Combine the vegetables in a large serving bowl and toss to mix. Pour over the dressing and toss until the vegetables are well coated. Leave to chill.

6 Just before serving, place the sunflower seeds on a baking tray and toast them in the oven or under the grill (broiler) until golden brown.

7 Scatter the sesame seeds over the coleslaw and serve.

COOK'S TIP

You can make coleslaw a few days in advance. To ensure that the sunflower seeds are crispy, add them just before serving.

VARIATION

For a slightly different taste, add one or more of the following ingredients to the coleslaw: raisins, grapes, grated apple, chopped walnuts, cubes of cheese or roasted peanuts.

Green Bean & Carrot Salad

*This colourful salad of crisp vegetables is
tossed in a delicious sun-dried tomato dressing.*

Serves 4

INGREDIENTS

350 g/12 oz green (French) beans	DRESSING:	1/4 tsp caster (superfine) sugar
225 g/8 oz carrots	2 tbsp extra virgin olive oil	salt and pepper
1 red (bell) pepper	1 tbsp red wine vinegar	
1 red onion	2 tsp sun-dried tomato paste	

1 Top and tail the beans and blanch them in boiling water for 4 minutes, until just tender. Drain the beans and rinse them under cold water until they are cool. Drain again thoroughly.

2 Transfer the beans to a large salad bowl.

3 Peel the carrots and cut them into thin matchsticks, using a mandolin if you have one.

4 Halve and deseed the (bell) pepper and cut the flesh into thin strips.

5 Peel the onion and cut it into thin slices.

6 Add the carrot, (bell) pepper and onion to the beans and toss to mix.

7 To make the dressing, place the oil, wine vinegar, sun-dried tomato paste, sugar and salt and pepper to taste in a small screw-top jar and shake well.

8 Pour the dressing over the vegetables and serve immediately or leave to chill in the refrigerator until required.

COOK'S TIP

*Use canned beans if fresh ones are
unavailable. Rinse off the salty
liquid and drain well. There is no
need to blanch canned beans.*

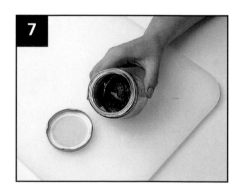

Spinach & Orange Salad

This is a refreshing and very nutritious salad. Add the dressing just before serving so that the leaves do not become soggy.

Serves 4-6

INGREDIENTS

225 g/8 oz baby spinach leaves
2 large oranges
1/2 red onion

DRESSING:
3 tbsp extra virgin olive oil
2 tbsp freshly squeezed orange juice
2 tsp lemon juice

1 tsp clear honey
1/2 tsp wholegrain mustard
salt and pepper

1 Wash the spinach leaves under cold running water and then dry them thoroughly on absorbent kitchen paper. Remove any tough stalks and tear the larger leaves into smaller pieces.

2 Slice the top and bottom off each orange with a sharp knife, then remove the peel.

3 Carefully slice between the membranes of the orange to remove the segments.

4 Using a sharp knife, finely chop the onion.

5 Mix together the salad leaves and orange segments and arrange in a serving dish.

6 Scatter the chopped onion over the salad.

7 To make the dressing, whisk together the olive oil, orange juice, lemon juice, honey, mustard and salt and pepper to taste in a small bowl.

8 Pour the dressing over the salad just before serving. Toss the salad well to coat the leaves with the dressing.

COOK'S TIP

Tear the spinach leaves into bite-sized pieces rather than cutting them because cutting bruises the leaves.

VARIATION

Use a mixture of spinach and watercress leaves, if you prefer a slightly more peppery flavour.

Potato Salad

You can use left-over cold potatoes, cut into bite-size pieces, for this salad. If you are making it from scratch, use tiny new potatoes for maximum flavour.

Serves 4

INGREDIENTS

700 g/1 lb 9 oz tiny new potatoes
8 spring onions (scallions)
1 hard-boiled (hard-cooked) egg
  (optional)

250 ml/9 fl oz/1 cup mayonnaise
1 tsp paprika
salt and pepper

TO GARNISH:
2 tbsp chives, snipped
pinch of paprika

1 Bring a large pan of lightly salted water to the boil. Add the potatoes to the pan and cook for 10–15 minutes or until they are just tender.

2 Drain the potatoes in a colander and rinse them under cold running water until they are completely cold. Drain them again thoroughly. Transfer the potatoes to a mixing bowl and set aside until required.

3 Using a sharp knife, trim and slice the spring onions (scallions) thinly on the diagonal.

4 Chop the hard-boiled (hard-cooked) egg, if using.

5 Combine the mayonnaise, paprika and salt and pepper to taste in a bowl. Pour the mixture over the potatoes.

6 Add the spring onions (scallions) and egg (if using) to the potatoes and toss together.

7 Transfer the potato salad to a serving bowl, sprinkle with snipped chives and a pinch of paprika. Cover and leave to chill in the refrigerator until required.

VARIATION

To make a lighter dressing, use a mixture of half mayonnaise and half natural yogurt.

VARIATION

Add cubes of cheese to the potato salad, if liked.

Tabouleh

*The fresh crunchy texture of this popular Middle Eastern
dish is perfect with barbecued (grilled) foods.*

Serves 4

INGREDIENTS

225 g/8 oz/2 cups cracked wheat
225 g/8 oz tomatoes
1 small onion
1/4 cucumber

1/2 red (bell) pepper
4 tbsp chopped, fresh parsley
3 tbsp chopped, fresh mint
2 tbsp pine nuts

4 tbsp lemon juice
4 tbsp extra virgin olive oil
2 cloves garlic, crushed
salt and pepper

1 Place the cracked wheat in a large bowl and cover with plenty of boiling water. Leave to stand for about 30 minutes or until the grains are tender and have swelled in size.

2 Drain the wheat through a large sieve. Press down with a plate in order to remove as much water as possible. Transfer the wheat to a large mixing bowl.

3 Cut the tomatoes in half, scoop out the seeds and discard them. Chop the flesh into fine dice.

4 Using a sharp knife, finely chop the onion.

5 Scoop out the seeds from the cucumber and discard them. Finely dice the cucumber flesh.

6 Deseed the (bell) peppers and chop the flesh.

7 Add the prepared vegetables to the wheat with the herbs and pine nuts. Toss until mixed.

8 Mix together the lemon juice oil, garlic and salt and pepper to taste in a small bowl.

9 Pour the mixture over the wheat and vegetables and toss together. Leave to chill in the refrigerator until required.

COOK'S TIP

This salad is best made a few hours before it is required to allow time for the flavours to develop and blend together. It can even be made a few days ahead, if wished.

Hot Lentil Salad with Balsamic Dressing

*A robust vinaigrette dressing is served with this warm salad.
If you prefer, you can serve the salad cold.*

Serves 6–8

INGREDIENTS

175 g/6 oz Puy lentils, cooked
4 tbsp olive oil
1 small onion, sliced
4 sticks celery, sliced
2 cloves garlic, crushed

2 courgettes (zucchini), trimmed and diced
125 g/4 $^1/_2$ oz green (French) beans, trimmed and cut into short lengths
$^1/_2$ red (bell) pepper, deseeded and diced

$^1/_2$ yellow (bell) pepper, deseeded and diced
1 tsp Dijon mustard
1 tbsp balsamic vinegar
salt and pepper

1 Place the lentils in a large mixing or serving bowl. The lentils can still be warm, if wished.

2 Heat the oil in a saucepan and fry the onion and celery for 2–3 minutes until softened but not browned.

3 Stir the garlic, courgettes (zucchini) and green (French) beans into the pan and cook for a further 2 minutes.

4 Add the (bell) peppers to the pan and cook for 1 minute.

5 Stir the mustard and the balsamic vinegar into the pan and mix until warm and well combined.

6 Pour the warm mixture over the lentils and toss together to mix well. Season with salt and pepper to taste and serve immediately.

COOK'S TIP

To cook the lentils, rinse them well and place in a large saucepan. Cover with plenty of cold water and bring to the boil. Boil rapidly for 10 minutes, then reduce the heat and simmer for 35 minutes until the lentils are tender. Drain well.

Italian Mozzarella Salad

This colourful salad is packed full of delicious flavours but is easy to make.

Serves 6

INGREDIENTS

200 g/7 oz baby spinach
125 g/4¹/₂ oz watercress
125 g/4¹/₂ oz Mozzarella cheese

225 g/8 oz cherry tomatoes
2 tsp balsamic vinegar
1¹/₂ tbsp extra virgin olive oil

salt and freshly ground black pepper

1 Wash the spinach and watercress and drain thoroughly on absorbent kitchen paper. Remove any tough stalks. Place the spinach and watercress leaves in a serving dish.

2 Cut the Mozzarella into small pieces and scatter them over the spinach and watercress leaves.

3 Cut the cherry tomatoes in half and scatter them over the salad.

4 Sprinkle over the balsamic vinegar and oil, and season with salt and pepper to taste. Toss the mixture together to coat the leaves. Serve at once or leave to chill in the refrigerator until required.

COOK'S TIP

Mozzarella is a highly popular cheese. It is a soft, fresh cheese with a piquant flavour, traditionally made from water buffalo's milk. It is usually sold surrounded by whey to keep it moist. Buffalo milk is now scarce, and so nowadays this cheese is often made with cow's milk. Mozzarella combines well with tomatoes, and this combination is now a classic.

VARIATION

Include Feta or Halloumi cheese instead of Mozzarella for a change, and use sherry vinegar instead of balsamic vinegar, if preferred.

Artichoke & Parma Ham (Prosciutto) Salad

This elegant starter would make a good first course. Serve it with a little fresh bread for mopping up the juices.

Serves 4

INGREDIENTS

275 g/9¹/₂ oz can artichoke hearts in oil, drained
4 small tomatoes
25 g/1 oz sun-dried tomatoes in oil
40 g/1¹/₂ oz Parma ham (prosciutto)

25 g/1 oz pitted black olives, halved
few basil leaves

DRESSING:
3 tbsp olive oil

1 tbsp white wine vinegar
1 clove garlic, crushed
¹/₂ tsp mild mustard
1 tsp clear honey
salt and pepper

1 Make sure the artichokes hearts are thoroughly drained, then cut them into quarters and place in a bowl.

2 Cut each fresh tomato into wedges. Slice the sun-dried tomatoes into thin strips. Cut the Parma ham (prosciutto) into thin strips and add to the bowl with the tomatoes and olive halves.

3 Keeping a few basil leaves whole for garnishing, tear the remainder of the leaves into small pieces and add to the bowl containing the other salad ingredients.

4 To make the dressing, put the oil, wine vinegar, garlic, mustard, honey and salt and pepper to taste in a screw-top jar and shake vigorously until the ingredients are well blended.

5 Pour the dressing over the salad and toss together.

6 Serve the salad garnished with a few whole basil leaves.

COOK'S TIP

Use bottled artichokes in oil if you can find them as they have a better flavour. If only canned artichokes are available, rinse them carefully to remove the salty liquid.

Pear & Roquefort Salad

The sweetness of the pear is a perfect partner to the 'bite' of the radiccio.

Serves 4

INGREDIENTS

50 g/1³/₄ oz Roquefort cheese
150 ml/5 fl oz/²/₃ cup low-fat natural
   yogurt
2 tbsp snipped chives

few leaves of lollo rosso
few leaves of radiccio
few leaves of lamb's lettuce (corn
   salad)

2 ripe pears
pepper
whole chives, to garnish

---

1 Place the cheese in a bowl and mash with a fork. Gradually blend the yogurt into the cheese to make a smooth dressing. Add the chives and season with pepper to taste.

2 Tear the lollo rosso, radiccio and lamb's lettuce leaves into manageable pieces. Arrange the salad leaves on a serving platter or on individual serving plates.

3 Quarter and core the pears and then cut them into slices.

4 Arrange the pear slices over the salad leaves.

5 Drizzle the dressing over the pears and garnish with a few whole chives. Serve at once.

COOK'S TIP

Look out for bags of mixed salad leaves as these are generally more economical than buying lots of different leaves separately. If you are using leaves that have not been prewashed, rinse them well and dry them thoroughly on absorbent paper kitchen towels or in a salad spinner. Alternatively, wrap the leaves in a clean tea towel (dish cloth) and shake dry.

COOK'S TIP

Arrange the Pear and Roquefort Salad on individual plates for an attractive starter, or on one large serving platter for a side salad.

Pasta Salad with Basil Vinaigrette

*All the ingredients of pesto sauce are included in this salad, which
has a fabulous summery taste, perfect for alfresco eating.*

Serves 4

INGREDIENTS

225 g/8 oz fusilli (pasta spirals)
4 tomatoes
50 g/1³/₄ oz black olives
25 g/1 oz sun-dried tomatoes in oil
2 tbsp pine nuts

2 tbsp grated Parmesan cheese
fresh basil, to garnish

VINAIGRETTE:
15 g/¹/₂ oz basil leaves

1 clove garlic
2 tbsp grated Parmesan cheese
4 tbsp extra virgin olive oil
2 tbsp lemon juice
salt and pepper

1 Cook the pasta in lightly salted boiling water for 10–12 minutes until just tender, or according to the instructions on the packet. Drain the pasta, rinse under cold water, then drain again thoroughly. Place the pasta in a large bowl.

2 To make the vinaigrette, place the basil leaves, garlic, cheese, oil and lemon juice in a food processor. Season with salt and pepper to taste. Process until the leaves are well chopped and the ingredients are combined.

Alternatively, finely chop the basil leaves by hand and combine with the other vinaigrette ingredients. Pour the vinaigrette over the pasta and toss to coat.

3 Cut the tomatoes into wedges. Pit and halve the olives. Slice the sun-dried tomatoes. Toast the pine nuts on a baking tray under the grill (broiler) until golden.

4 Add the tomatoes (fresh and sun-dried) and the olives to the pasta and mix until combined.

5 Transfer the pasta to a serving dish, scatter over the Parmesan and pine nuts and garnish with a few basil leaves.

COOK'S TIP

Sun-dried tomatoes have a strong, intense flavour. They are most frequently found packed in oil with herbs and garlic. Do not waste the oil, which has an excellent flavour, instead use it in salad dressings.

Mango & Wild Rice Salad

*Wild rice is, in fact, an aquatic grass that is native to North America.
It has a delicious nutty flavour and a slightly chewy texture.*

Serves 6

INGREDIENTS

75 g/2³/₄ oz/¹/₂ cup wild rice
150 g/5¹/₂ oz/1 cup Basmati rice
3 tbsp hazelnut oil
1 tbsp sherry vinegar
1 ripe mango

3 sticks celery
75 g/2³/₄ oz ready-to-eat dried
　apricots, chopped
75 g/2³/₄ oz flaked (slivered)
　almonds, flaked

2 tbsp chopped, fresh coriander
　(cilantro) or mint
salt and pepper
sprigs of fresh coriander (cilantro) or
　mint, to garnish

1 Cook the rice in separate saucepans in lightly salted boiling water. Cook the wild rice for 45–50 minutes and the Basmati rice for 10–12 minutes. Drain, rinse well and drain again. Place the rice in a large bowl.

2 Mix the oil, vinegar and seasoning together. Pour the mixture over the rice and toss well.

3 Cut the mango in half lengthwise, as close to the stone as possible. Remove and discard the stone.

4 Peel the skin from the mango and cut the flesh into slices.

5 Slice the celery thinly and add to the cooled rice with the mango, apricots, almonds and chopped herbs. Toss together and transfer to a serving dish. Garnish with sprigs of of fresh herbs.

COOK'S TIP

Add dressings to rice salads while the rice is still hot because the rice will absorb the flavour better.

COOK'S TIP

To toast almonds, place them on a baking sheet in a preheated oven 180°C/350°F/Gas Mark 4 for 5–10 minutes. Alternatively, toast them under the grill (broiler), turning frequently and keeping a close eye on them because they will quickly burn.

Mixed Bean Salad

Use a mixture of any canned beans in this crunchy, very filling salad.

Serves 6-8

INGREDIENTS

400 g/14 oz can flageolet (small navy) beans, drained
400 g/14 oz can red kidney beans, drained
400 g/14 oz can butter beans, drained

1 small red onion, thinly sliced
175 g/6 oz dwarf green beans, topped and tailed
1 red (bell) pepper, halved and deseeded

DRESSING:
4 tbsp olive oil
2 tbsp sherry vinegar
2 tbsp lemon juice
1 tsp light muscovado sugar
1 tsp chilli sauce (optional)

1 Put the canned beans in a large mixing bowl. Add the sliced onion and mix together.

2 Cut the dwarf green beans in half and cook in lightly salted boiling water for about 8 minutes until just tender. Refresh under cold water and drain again. Add to the mixed beans and onions.

3 Place the (bell) pepper halves, cut side down, on a grill (broiler) rack and cook until the skin blackens and chars. Leave to cool slightly then pop them into a plastic bag for about 10 minutes. Peel away the skin from the (bell) peppers and discard. Roughly chop the (bell) pepper flesh and add it to the beans.

4 To make the dressing, place the oil, sherry vinegar, lemon juice, sugar and chilli sauce (if using) in a screw-top jar and shake vigorously.

5 Pour the dressing over the mixed bean salad and toss well. Leave to chill in the refrigerator until required.

VARIATION

You can use any combination of beans in this salad. For a distinctive flavour, add 1 teaspoon of curry paste instead of the chilli sauce.

VARIATION

Add some flaked tuna fish or garlic sausage to turn this side salad into a main meal.

Mediterranean (Bell) Pepper Salad

This salad is full of fabulous Mediterranean flavours and it goes well with all barbecued (grilled) foods, especially meats. Alternatively, serve it with a selection of French and Italian breads for a simple starter.

Serves 4

INGREDIENTS

2 red (bell) peppers, halved and deseeded
2 yellow (bell) peppers, halved and deseeded
3 tbsp extra virgin olive oil

1 onion, cut into wedges
2 large courgettes (zucchini), sliced
2 garlic cloves, sliced
1 tbsp balsamic vinegar
50 g/1³/4 oz anchovy fillets, chopped

25 g/1 oz pitted black olives, quartered
fresh basil leaves

1 Place the (bell) pepper halves, cut side down, on a grill (broiler) pan and cook until the skin blackens and chars. Leave to cool slightly then pop them into a plastic bag for about 10 minutes.

2 Peel away the skin from the (bell) peppers and discard. Cut the flesh into thick strips.

3 Heat the oil in a large frying pan (skillet), add the onion and cook gently for 10 minutes or until softened. Add the courgette (zucchini) slices, garlic and (bell) pepper strips to the pan and cook, stirring occasionally, for a further 10 minutes.

4 Add the vinegar, anchovies and olives to the pan. Season to taste. Mix well and leave to cool.

5 Reserve a few basil leaves for garnishing, then tear the remainder into small pieces. Stir them into the salad.

6 Transfer the salad to a serving dish and garnish with a few whole basil leaves.

COOK'S TIP

Balsamic vinegar is made in and around Modena in Italy. Its rich, mellow flavour is perfect for Mediterranean-style salads, but if it is unavailable, use sherry vinegar or white wine vinegar instead.

Desserts

Don't forget the dessert – it can be cooked on the barbecue (grill), too. Although desserts are not the most important part of a barbecue (grill) spread, they are always fun to cook and most can be prepared in advance and left above the cooling coals to cook to perfection while you tuck into the main course.

Fruit is always a good choice because it contrasts so well with the often rich and filling main courses. Try croissants filled with chocolate and raspberries or panettone topped with marscapone cheese.

Have plenty of ice cream as a stand-by. It's popular with the children and is delicious served with barbecued (grilled) fruits on a hot summer day. Thick natural yogurt or single (light) cream are also ideal accompaniments. If you don't want a hot dessert, prepare a simple fruit salad.

For a quick sweet treat thread marshmallows on to skewers and hold them above the warm coals until just softened. Alternatively, try threading cubes of teacake on to a skewer, toast until golden and serve with a little maple syrup.

Barbecued (Grilled) Baked Apples

When they are wrapped in kitchen foil, apples bake to perfection on the barbecue (grill) and make a delightful finale to any meal.

Serves 4

INGREDIENTS

4 medium cooking apples
25 g/1 oz walnuts, chopped
25 g/1 oz ground almonds
25 g/1 oz light muscovado sugar

25 g/1 oz cherries, chopped
25 g/1 oz stem ginger, chopped
1 tbsp amaretto (almond-flavoured liqueur) (optional)

50 g/1³/₄ oz butter
single (light) cream or natural yogurt, to serve

1 Core the apples and using a knife, score each one around the middle to prevent the apple skins from splitting during barbecueing (grilling).

2 To make the filling, mix together the walnuts, almonds, sugar, cherries, ginger and amaretto (almond-flavoured liqueur), if using, in a small bowl.

3 Spoon the filling mixture into each apple, pushing it down into the hollowed-out core. Mound a little of the filling mixture on top of each apple.

4 Place each apple on a large square of double thickness kitchen foil and generously dot all over with the butter. Wrap up the foil so that the apple is completely enclosed.

5 Barbecue (grill) the foil parcels containing the apples over hot coals for 25–30 minutes or until tender.

6 Transfer the apples to warm, individual serving plates. Serve with lashings of whipped single (light) cream or thick natural yogurt.

COOK'S TIP

If the coals are dying down, place the kitchen foil parcels directly on to the coals, raking them up around the apples. Barbecue (grill) for 25–30 minutes and serve with the cream or yogurt.

Fruity Skewers with Chocolate Dipping Sauce

*These warm, lightly barbecued (grilled) fruit kebabs (kabobs)
are served with a delicious chocolate dipping sauce.*

Serves 4

INGREDIENTS

Selection of fruit (choose from
  oranges, bananas, strawberries,
  pineapple chunks (fresh or canned),
  apricots (fresh or canned), dessert
  (eating) apples, pears, kiwi fruit)
1 tbsp lemon juice

CHOCOLATE SAUCE:
50 g/1³/₄ oz butter
50 g/1³/₄ oz plain (dark) chocolate,
  broken into small cubes
¹/₂ tbsp cocoa powder
2 tbsp golden syrup

BASTE:
4 tbsp clear honey
grated rind and juice of ¹/₂ orange

1 To make the chocolate sauce, place the butter, chocolate, cocoa powder and golden syrup in a small pan. Heat gently on a stove or at the side of the barbecue (grill), stirring continuously, until all of the ingredients have melted and are well combined.

2 To prepare the fruit, peel and core if necessary, then cut into large, bite-size pieces or wedges as appropriate. Dip apples, pears and bananas in lemon juice to prevent discoloration. Thread the pieces of fruit on to skewers.

3 To make the baste, mix together the honey, orange juice and rind, heat gently if required and brush over the fruit.

4 Barbecue (grill) the fruit skewers over warm coals for 5–10 minutes until hot. Serve with the chocolate dipping sauce.

COOK'S TIP

If the coals are too hot raise the rack so that it is about 15 cm/ 6 inches above the coals or spread out the coals a little to reduce the heat. Do not assemble the fruit skewers more than 1–2 hours before they are required.

Toffee Fruit Kebabs (Kabobs)

Serve these fruit kebabs (kabobs) with a sticky toffee sauce. They are perfect for autumn barbecues (grills) such as Hallowe'en or Bonfire Night.

Serves 4

INGREDIENTS

2 dessert (eating) apples, cored and cut into wedges

2 firm pears, cored and cut into wedges

juice of $^1/_2$ lemon

25 g/1 oz light muscovado sugar

$^1/_4$ tsp ground allspice

25 g/1 oz unsalted butter, melted

SAUCE:

125 g/4$^1/_2$ oz butter

100 g/3$^1/_2$ oz light muscovado sugar

6 tbsp double (heavy) cream

1 Toss the apple and pears in the lemon juice to prevent any discoloration.

2 Mix the sugar and allspice together and sprinkle over the fruit.

3 Thread the fruit pieces on to skewers.

4 To make the toffee sauce, place the butter and sugar in a saucepan and heat, stirring gently, until the butter has melted and the sugar has dissolved.

5 Add the cream to the saucepan and bring to the boil. Boil for 1–2 minutes, then set aside to cool slightly.

6 Meanwhile, place the fruit kebabs (kabobs) over hot coals and barbecue (grill) for about 5 minutes, turning and basting frequently with the melted butter, until the fruit is just tender.

7 Transfer the fruit kebabs (kabobs) to warm serving plates and serve with the slightly cooled toffee sauce.

COOK'S TIP

Firm apples that will keep their shape are needed for this dish – varieties such as Golden Delicious, Granny Smith and Braeburn are a good choice. Soft apples and pears will become mushy as they cook.

VARIATION

Sprinkle the fruit kebabs (kabobs) with chopped walnuts or pecan nuts before serving, if you wish.

Chocolate & Raspberry Croissants

*Simple to prepare, these tasty croissants are popped on the barbecue (grill)
to warm through until the chocolate melts.*

Serves 4

INGREDIENTS

4 butter croissants	75 g/2 ³/₄ oz plain (dark) chocolate	oil, for greasing
4 tsp raspberry preserve	125 g/ 4¹/₂ oz raspberries	

1 Slice the croissants in half. Spread the bottom half of each croissant with 1 teaspoon of the raspberry preserve.

2 Grate or finely chop the chocolate and sprinkle over the raspberry preserve.

3 Lightly grease 4 sheets of kitchen foil, brushing with a little oil.

4 Divide the raspberries equally among the croissants and replace the top half of each croissant. Place each croissant on to a sheet of foil, wrapping the foil to enclose the croissant completely.

5 Place the rack 15 cm/6 inches above hot coals. Transfer the croissants to the rack and leave them to heat through for 10–15 minutes or until the chocolate just begins to melt.

6 Remove the foil and transfer the croissants to individual serving plates. Serve hot.

VARIATION

For a delicious chocolate and strawberry filling for the croissants, use sliced strawberries and strawberry preserve instead of the raspberries.

VARIATION

You could also use milk chocolate or a mixture of milk and plain (dark) chocolate for this dish.

COOK'S TIP

Use the best quality fruit preserve you can find. Better still, use homemade jams and preserves.

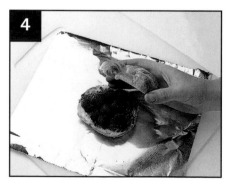

Baked Bananas

The orange-flavoured cream can be prepared in advance but do not make up the banana parcels until just before you need to barbecue (grill) them – they take only a few moments to get ready.

Serves 4

INGREDIENTS

4 bananas
2 passion fruit
4 tbsp orange juice
4 tbsp orange-flavoured liqueur

ORANGE-FLAVOURED CREAM:
150 ml/5 fl oz/ $^2/_3$ cup double (heavy) cream
3 tbsp icing (confectioners') sugar

2 tbsp orange-flavoured liqueur

1 Peel the bananas and place each one on to a sheet of kitchen foil.

2 Cut the passion fruit in half and squeeze the juice of each half over each banana. Spoon over the orange juice and liqueur.

3 Fold the kitchen foil over the top of the bananas to enclose the bananas completely.

4 Barbecue (grill) the bananas over hot coals for about 10 minutes or until the bananas are just tender.

5 To make the orange-flavoured cream, pour the double (heavy) cream into a mixing bowl and sprinkle over the icing (confectioners') sugar. Whisk the mixture until it is standing in soft peaks. Carefully fold in the orange-flavoured liqueur and leave to chill in the refrigerator until required.

6 Transfer the foil parcels to warm, individual serving plates. Open out the foil parcels at the table and then serve immediately with the orange-flavoured cream.

VARIATION

Leave the bananas in their skins for a really quick dessert. Split the banana skins and pop in 1–2 cubes of chocolate. Wrap the bananas in kitchen foil and barbecue (grill) for 10 minutes, or until the chocolate just melts.

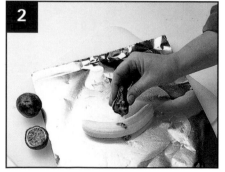

Panettone with Mascarpone & Strawberries

Panettone is a sweet Italian bread. It is delicious toasted, and when it is topped with marscapone cheese and marinated strawberries it makes a sumptuous dessert.

Serves 4

INGREDIENTS

225 g/8 oz strawberries
25 g/1 oz caster (superfine) sugar

6 tbsp Marsala wine
1/2 tsp ground cinnamon

4 slices panettone
4 tbsp mascarpone cheese

1 Hull and slice the strawberries and place them in a bowl. Add the sugar, Marsala and cinnamon to the strawberries.

2 Toss the strawberries in the sugar and cinnamon mixture until they are well coated. Leave to chill in the refrigerator for at least 30 minutes.

3 When ready to serve, transfer the slices of panettone to a rack set over medium hot coals. Barbecue (grill) the panettone for about 1 minute on each side or until golden brown.

4 Remove the panettone from the barbecue (grill) and transfer to serving plates. Top the panettone with the mascarpone cheese and the marinated strawberries. Serve immediately.

COOK'S TIP

Mascarpone is an Italian soft cheese with a rich, creamy texture, which tastes like very thick cream. It will melt into the panettone, making it quite delicious. If mascarpone is unavailable, clotted cream would be a good alternative.

VARIATION

Spread mascarpone cheese on to teacakes that have been toasted on the barbecue (grill).

Pina Colada Pineapple

The flavours of pineapple and coconut blend well together, as they do in the well-known drink Pina Colada. Here, barbecued (grilled) pineapple is served with coconut for an equally special effect.

Serves 4

INGREDIENTS

1 small pineapple
50 g/1¾ oz unsalted butter

25 g/1 oz light muscovado sugar
50 g/1¾ oz fresh coconut, grated

2 tbsp coconut-flavoured liqueur or rum

1 Using a very sharp knife, cut the pineapple into quarters and then remove the tough core from the centre, leaving the leaves attached.

2 Carefully cut the pineapple flesh away from the skin. Make horizontal cuts across the flesh of the pineapple quarters.

3 Place the butter in a pan and heat gently until melted, stirring continuously. Brush the melted butter over the pineapple and sprinkle with the sugar.

4 Cover the pineapple leaves with kitchen foil in order to prevent them from burning and transfer them to a rack set over hot coals.

5 Barbecue (grill) the pineapple for about 10 minutes.

6 Sprinkle the coconut over the pineapple and barbecue (grill), cut side up, for a further 5–10 minutes or until the pineapple is piping hot.

7 Transfer the pineapple to serving plates and remove the foil from the leaves. Spoon a little coconut-flavoured liqueur or rum over the pineapple and serve immediately.

COOK'S TIP

Fresh coconut has the best flavour for this dish. If you prefer, however, you can use desiccated (shredded) coconut.

Stuffed Pears with Mincemeat

Pears quickly go soft and lose their shape when they are cooked,
so choose fruit with good firm flesh for this recipe.

Serves 4

INGREDIENTS

4 firm pears
1 tsp lemon juice
2 tbsp mincemeat

5 tbsp cake crumbs or 4 amaretti
  biscuits, crushed

15 g/¹/₂ oz butter
ice cream, to serve

1 Using a sharp knife, cut the pears in half. Using a teaspoon, scoop out the core and discard.

2 Brush the cut surface of each of the pear halves with a little lemon juice to prevent discoloration.

3 Mix together the mincemeat and cake crumbs or crushed amaretti biscuits.

4 Divide the mixture among the pear halves, spooning it into a mound where the core has been removed.

5 Place 2 pear halves on a large square of double thickness kitchen foil and generously dot all over with the butter.

6 Wrap up the foil around the pears so that they are completely enclosed.

7 Transfer the foil parcels to a rack set over hot coals. Barbecue (grill) for 25–30 minutes or until the pears are hot and just tender.

8 Transfer the pears to individual serving plates. Serve with 2 scoops of ice cream per serving.

VARIATION

Use mincemeat to stuff apples instead of pears and bake them on the barbecue (grill) in the same way.

COOK'S TIP

If the coals are dying down, place the kitchen foil parcels directly on to the coals and barbecue (grill) for 25–30 minutes.

Peaches with Creamy Mascarpone Filling

If you prepare these in advance, all you have to do is pop the peaches on the barbecue (grill) when you are ready to serve them.

Serves 4

INGREDIENTS

4 peaches
175 g/6 oz mascarpone cheese

40 g/1^1/$_2$ oz pecan or walnuts, chopped

1 tsp sunflower oil
4 tbsp maple syrup

1 Cut the peaches in half and remove the stones. If you are preparing this recipe in advance, press the peach halves together again and wrap them in cling film (plastic wrap) until required.

2 Mix the mascarpone and pecan or walnuts together in a small bowl until well combined. Leave to chill in the refrigerator until required.

3 To serve, brush the peaches with a little oil and place on a rack set over medium hot coals. Barbecue (grill) the peach halves for 5–10 minutes, turning once, until hot.

4 Transfer the peach halves to a serving dish and top with the mascarpone and nut mixture.

5 Drizzle the maple syrup over the peaches and mascarpone filling and serve at once.

VARIATION

You can use nectarines instead of peaches for this recipe, if you prefer. Remember to choose ripe but fairly firm fruit which won't go soft and mushy when it is barbecued (grilled). Prepare the nectarines in the same way as the peaches and barbecue (grill) for 5–10 minutes.

COOK'S TIP

Mascarpone cheese is high in fat, so if you are following a low-fat diet, use thick natural yogurt instead.

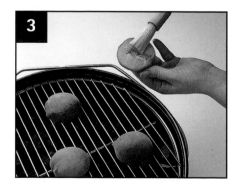

Exotic Fruity Parcels

Delicious pieces of exotic fruit are warmed through in a deliciously scented, pomegranate-flavoured sauce to make a fabulous barbecue (grill) dessert.

Serves 4

INGREDIENTS

1 pawpaw (papaya)	1 tbsp grenadine	single (light) cream or natural yogurt,
1 mango	3 tbsp orange juice	to serve
1 star fruit		

1 Cut the pawpaw (papaya) in half, scoop out the seeds and discard them. Peel the pawpaw (papaya) and cut the flesh into thick slices.

2 Prepare the mango by cutting it lengthwise in half either side of the central stone.

3 Score each mango half in a criss-cross pattern. Push each mango half inside out to separate the cubes and cut them away from the peel.

4 Using a sharp knife, thickly slice the star fruit.

5 Place all of the fruit in a bowl and mix them together.

6 Mix the grenadine and orange juice together and pour over the fruit. Leave to marinate for at least 30 minutes.

7 Divide the fruit among 4 double thickness squares of kitchen foil and gather up the edges to form a parcel that encloses the fruit.

8 Place the foil parcel on a rack set over warm coals and barbecue (grill) the fruit for 15–20 minutes.

9 Serve the fruit in the parcel, with single (light) cream or yogurt offered separately.

COOK'S TIP

Grenadine is a sweet syrup made from pomegranates. If you prefer you could use pomegranate juice instead of the grenadine for this recipe. To extract the juice, cut the pomegranate in half and squeeze gently with a lemon squeezer – do not press too hard or the juice may become bitter.

Index

Index compiled by Hilary Bird.